BOOK OF FOOLS

The Fool is understood as a kind of Everyperson: the human personality in its sweetest, simplest, most innocent, most impetuous, most courageous state. Yes, the term will make you cringe, but he (and she, of course), is the Inner Child. An earlier generation also liked the term *Puer Aeternus*, Eternal Child, although this was also used as a psychological diagnosis for an adult with commitment problems (before we came to understand that we no longer have problems, but instead "issues"). The Fool's Journey is also the name given to a favorite approach to the tarot, as the trump sequence is seen as a path of lessons, obstacles, and pleasures that the Fool encounters on life's adventure. Almost all of us can identify with the innocence, the fresh start, represented by the Fool—and those few people who can't appreciate the Fool probably need his influence most.

About the Author

Brian Williams was an artist, author, tarot lecturer, and Italian expert who brought twenty-five years of experience and study to these related disciplines. He held a B.A. in Italian Renaissance Iconographic Studies from the University of California, Berkeley. He had studied in Italy, and was artist-in-residence at the Istituto nazionale della grafica, Calcografia in Rome in 1984–85. He was a respected expert in the history and symbolism of the tarot, as well as one of America's most prominent and prolific tarot artists.

Williams was a frequent speaker and presenter at tarot organization events and meetings, and led tarot-focused educational/celebratory tours to Italy.

To Write to the Author

If you would like more information about this book, please write to Llewellyn Worldwide and we will address your request. The publisher appreciates hearing from you and learning of your enjoyment of this book. Please write to:

Llewellyn Worldwide
P.O. Box 64383, Dept. 0-7387-0161-0
St. Paul, MN 55164-0383, U.S.A.

Please include a self-addressed, stamped envelope with your letter.
If outside the U.S.A., enclose international postal coupons.

Many of Llewellyn's authors have websites with additional information and resources. For more information, please visit our website at www.llewellyn.com.

Book
of Fools

Brian Williams

2002
Llewellyn Publications
St. Paul, Minnesota 64383-0383, U.S.A.

FIRST EDITION
First Printing, 2002

Cover design by Lisa Novak
Cover art © 2001 by Brian Williams
Editing and interior design by Connie Hill
Illustrations from *Rider-Waite Tarot* deck (Copyright © 1993 by U.S. Games Systems, Inc.) and *Tarot Classic* (Copyright © 1971 by U.S. Games Systems, Inc.) reproduced by permission of U.S. Games Systems, Inc., Stamford, CT 06902 U.S.A. Further reproduction prohibited.

Library of Congress Cataloging-in-Publication Data
Williams, Brian, 1958–2002.
    Book of fools / inspired by the art of Sebastian Brant / Brian Williams. — 1st ed.
      p.   cm. —
    Includes bibliographical references.
    ISBN 0-7387-0161-0 (pbk)
   1. Tarot. I. Title.
BF1879.T2 W445   2002
133.3'2424—dc21   2002141559

Llewellyn Publications
A Division of Llewellyn Worldwide, Ltd.
P.O. Box 64383, Dept. 0–7387-0161-0
St. Paul, Minnesota 55164-0383, U.S.A.
http://www.llewellyn.com

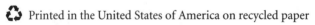 Printed in the United States of America on recycled paper

Of fools such tidings I did tell
So that all men would know
them well . . .

Also by Brian Williams

Renaissance Tarot, deck, U.S. Games, 1987

Renaissance Tarot, book, U.S. Games, 1994

PoMo (Postmodern) *Tarot*, deck and book, HarperCollins, 1994

Angel Journey, deck only (book by Terry Lynn Taylor and Mary Beth Crain), HarperCollins, 1996

The Light and Shadow Tarot, book only (art by Michael Goepferd), Destiny Books, 1997

The Minchiate Tarot, deck and book, Destiny Books, 1999

Table of Contents

Publisher's Note

Brian Williams passed away on April 15, 2002; The *Ship of Fools Tarot* was Brian's last work. His talent, knowledge, and charm will be greatly missed.

Acknowledgments

I'd like to thank first a trio of tarot goddesses, whom I am honored to call *amiche del cuore*, friends of the heart: Thalassa, mastermind and ringmistress of the San Francisco Bay Area Tarot Symposium; and the justly beloved and revered authors and teachers Rachel Pollack and Mary K. Greer. These three brilliant women have long inspired and delighted me, as they have so many others. I'd also like to thank Barbara Moore and the good people at Llewellyn for taking on this quirky project. Last but not least, my sincere thanks go to Peter Spoerl for his excellent translations of Sebastian Brant. I have in a few instances tinkered with his wording, but the task of rendering Brant's Middle German verses into lively English is entirely his accomplishment.

Introduction

Why a *Ship of Fools Tarot?* Why indeed! As the late Eden Gray asked rhetorically at a tarot gathering in Chicago, do we really need all these new versions of the tarot? My answer, then and now, is twofold. First, as an artist and designer, I can't help myself. Somehow, no matter how final my final tarot project may seem, another one (or another five) springs to mind and insists on being realized. This is well and good, but I might keep these new series to myself, as I'm certain many will say. The second part of the answer then is that one must hope that a new tarot will actually talk to others—and not merely artistically, or as a visual novelty, but as a vehicle for usable insights, ideas, and feelings. This is certainly my hope for this series.

Here then is an all-fools tarot. ("All fools, all the time!" as Madama Thalassa might say, tap-dancing and swinging ropes of jet beads.) This is a deck that may well speak to a part of the tarot-soul that hasn't yet been addressed. The Fool card of the tarot has emerged in recent decades as a pivotal figure of the deck. He is understood as a kind of Everyperson: the human personality in its sweetest, simplest, most innocent, most impetuous, most courageous state. Yes, the term will make you cringe, but he (and she, of course), is the Inner Child. An earlier generation also liked the term *Puer Aeternus*, Eternal Child, although this was also used as a psychological diagnosis for an adult with commitment problems (before we came to understand that we no longer have problems, but instead "issues"). The Fool's Journey is also the name given to a favorite approach to the tarot, as the trump sequence is seen as a path of lessons, obstacles, and pleasures that the Fool encounters on life's adventure. Almost all of us can identify with the innocence, the fresh start, represented by the Fool—and those few people who can't appreciate the Fool probably need his influence most.

The *Ship of Fools* is a new interpretation of the tarot, but one that is nonetheless a traditional tarot deck. That is, there are the customary seventy-eight cards, divided into two groups: the twenty-two trumps or Major Arcana, and the four additional suits, or Minor Arcana, similar in structure to modern playing cards, of Swords, Staves (sometimes called Wands), Cups, and Coins (or Pentacles). The twenty-two trumps of the *Ship of Fools Tarot* include the classic subjects and ideas—with, as we'll see, some dramatic departures. The fourteen cards of each of the four suits also follow the traditional tarot structure, with numbered cards, or pips, from Ace through Ten, and court cards of Page, Knight, Queen, and King.

The *Ship of Fools Tarot* was born in a curious way. I had long been familiar with Sebastian Brant's masterpiece of German literature, *Das Narrenschiff*, or *The Ship of Fools*. Over the years I have occasionally referred to the *Narrenschiff* in my books and in talks at tarot conferences. Brant's text is funny and biting, yet humane. The woodcut images are some of the most delightful book illustrations ever created. Several of the best are the work of the young Albrecht Dürer, who was in Basel in the period before the book's publication, in 1494, by a gentleman printer named Johann Bergmann von Olpe.

The relevance of the *Narrenschiff* to the tarot is in its capacity as a sort of Renaissance catalogue or register. The *Narrenschiff* images and text function as a kind of encyclopedia of the human soul, with special emphasis on humanity's capacity for foolishness. In this way it echoes, however remotely, the tarot series, with its intriguing elements of hierarchy and category, of classification and encapsulation. There are many other such European series, of course, with potential echoes in the tarot. Remaining in the German Renaissance, for instance, we find such works as Hans Holbein's magnificent woodcut series of the *Dance of Death*, or *Totentanz*; and Jost Amman's *Book of Trades*, or *Ständebuch*, in which the professions and "estates" of humanity are set out in sequence from Pope down to Simpleton. Holbein's series would make, with some adjustments, a spectacular "Dance of Death Tarot," just as Amman's images could be so transformed.

The striking thing about the Narrenschiff, similarly, is that fifteen or sixteen of the twenty-two tarot trumps can be found, readymade, among the one hundred or so woodcut illustrations, and almost all the remaining half-dozen images can be concocted from *Narrenschiff* originals with only the slightest adjustments. This is not to suggest that there is any material connection between the tarot trumps, a series invented before 1450, and attached to the four-suit playing card deck in northern Italy, and Brant's late fifteenth-century German book. This coincidence suggests instead the point that I have attempted to make many times in the past, in books and talks, that the archetypal images of the tarot have parallels and echoes everywhere in medieval and Renaissance culture.

Inspired then by this curious accordance of the *Narrenschiff* and the tarot, I plunged into designing a *Ship of Fools Tarot*, following the original images line-for-line for some cards, and concocting others—assembling details from more than one image. For the trumps, especially, I have tried to be as faithful as possible to both the *Narrenschiff* illustrations and to early tarot iconography. The four suits, on the other hand, posed a different set of pleasures and challenges. To be faithful to early tarot tradition here would have meant designing simple arrangements of suit signs for the pips, and straightforward kings and queens for the courts. Scenes on the numbered cards of the tarot date only, after all, to the early twentieth-century images that artist Pamela Colman Smith created for author Alfred Edward Waite. Between the richness of Brant's illustrations on one hand, and the charm—and esoteric precedent—of the *Waite-Smith* cards on the other, I decided to assemble a Minor Arcana to reflect the influence of both. Some cards then come directly from Brant, and have no connection to anything else, but many others are inspired directly by the images and ideas of *Waite-Smith*. This, I hope, will be a source of interest and amusement to a reader familiar with the *Waite-Smith* deck and its descendants, as parallels and transpositions from *Waite-Smith* pop up in this German Renaissance context.

The following chapters discuss the *Ship of Fools* cards one by one, in the following way: first the card itself is described; then it is compared to its *Narrenschiff* source image, when there is one; finally a comparison is made with the corresponding cards from the *Tarot de Marseille* and the *Waite-Smith* decks. The *Ship of Fools Tarot* can thus be placed firmly in the context of tarot history and tradition, and at the same time this book can serve, for the beginner, as a sort of introduction to tarot imagery and meaning in general. For the tarot adept these comparisons should render transparent the decisions, artistic and symbolic, that the author has made in designing this series.

An excellent source for Brant's *Narrenschiff* is the Dover reprint of Zeydel's 1944 classic translation and commentary. Here is everything needed: all of the original illustrations from the definitive early editions; all chapters and chapter headings translated, with great wit and imagination; and a thoroughly readable scholarly rundown of the book's origins, fortunes, and legacy. I consulted Zeydel with pleasure, but turned to a few nineteenth-century volumes for the definitive German text and for the images themselves. Zarncke's critical edition of 1854 provided me with the passages, which I then asked Berkeley scholar Peter Spoerl to translate. These are more literal translations than Professor Zeydel's charming rhymes, but may therefore be expected to be closer to the *Narrenschiff*—including, incidentally, when Brant is crude in a way that couldn't be published in the 1944 edition. For the original images I turned to the handsome facsimile *Narrenschiff* published by Schultz in 1913.

The figure of the fool was not original with Brant, of course; instead it descends from the earliest memories of culture, from mythology and scripture. *Fastnachtspiele* may have directly influenced Brant, as these Shrovetide or Carnival plays included capering fools. The fabled Land of Cockayne, a legendary realm of happy, slothful carousers, was a favorite motif of medieval literature. Even the idea of a crew of fools crowding a ship was not Brant's invention, as scholars have found a few Dutch and German precedents. The most immediate and telling prior instance of a fools' ship like Brant's is a published sermon discovered by Adolf Spamer: "In his sermon this preacher describes twenty-one fools of the 'Narrenschiff' and, as the twenty-second character, Christ, who followed by St. Ursula's ship, crosses the sea dry and exhorts the fools to leave their vessel and board Christ's St. Ursula's ship, which is described as a ship of penitence" (p. 13, Zeydel). Here, coincidentally, is a surprising structural correspondence with the tarot trumps: twenty-one characters, like the twenty-one trumps, joined by a twenty-second figure, an odd-man-out. In the tarot this wild card is the Fool; in the German sermon he is Christ.

Brant's book was tremendously influential in European letters, for centuries, engendering dozens of translations (usually unreliable), and hundreds of editions (almost all unauthorized). Brant certainly influenced the masterpiece of his younger contemporary, Erasmus of Rotterdam, who wrote his *Moriae encomium*, or *In Praise of Folly*, while staying with his learned English friend, Sir Thomas More, in 1509. The *Narrenschiff* remains a landmark of German language and culture to this day, but is only vaguely remembered in current English language letters. Even so there are memories of Brant in such disparate creations as a 1962 novel titled *The Ship of Fools* by Katherine Anne Porter, on which was based the 1965 Hollywood film, and in similarly titled songs by such bands as the Doors and the Grateful Dead.

The source used for the cards of the *Tarot de Marseille* is a deck called *Tarot Classic*, published by U.S. Games Systems. In this particular case the cards have Italian titles, although, as the name suggests, this traditional tarot is associated with France in general and the city of Marseilles, an old center of card printing, in particular. Also from U.S. Games come the versions of the deck designed for A. E. Waite. Rider was the pack's first publisher; Waite was its inventor; Smith was its artist. The deck has therefore been called the *Waite* deck, the *Rider-Waite*, even the *Rider*. I have chosen here to use the term "Waite-Smith," especially as it has become so clear that Pamela Colman Smith's contribution to the result was much more than that of a passive conduit. Pixie Smith—in consultation, of course, with Waite—brought a great deal of her own ideas and insights to her attractive designs.

At the heart of the *Ship of Fools Tarot* lies an apparently irreconcilable paradox. Brant, at every turn, admonishes us *not* to be fools. He warns, exhorts, cajoles, and scolds. His is the conventional morality of an obedient pre-Reformation German Christian burgher. He is even philistine enough to put sins like adultery on the same level as inattention in church. He is learned and humane—a humanist in spite of himself. His writing is fun and very funny. But he is also perfectly stodgy at heart, a curmudgeon. He would disapprove, undoubtedly, of the point of view embodied in the *Ship of Fools Tarot*—for this is a series that, inspired by the vital images of Brant's book, aids and abets foolery.

These two tendencies can indeed be reconciled—with a little moral tap dancing. It is possible to hear, and heed, Brant's blandishments, and at the same time enjoy, and even feel inspired by, the insouciance and courage of his fools. It is possible, even necessary, to entertain both points of view at once. Of course we must conduct ourselves in life with wisdom and restraint, but it is also vital that we remember the verve and lust for life of the Fool. For this reason I have happily included Brant's scolding lessons, even when they contradict the purpose I've imposed on an image. I can hear the objection that in proposing this balance I am being postmodern, an insult in some circles. Well, as the proud father of a publication called *PoMo Tarot*, I can hardly reject the term, or feel much burdened by it. Indeed, I'd like to embrace the label, with whatever funny baggage it may entail. I believe it is possible to embrace the tarot as both image and idea; as individual artistic expression and universal symbol; as historical artifact and mysterious phenomenon; as exoteric game and esoteric instrument. Seriousness and joy need not be mutually exclusive states! It should be possible to be the Fool—one hopes—and not be an idiot.

Brian Williams
Tarotier postmoderne

MAJOR ARCANA

0 — *The Vagabond*

0 THE VAGABOND

0-1, *Ship of Fools Tarot*

barefoot fool strides along a seashore while a little dog bites his tunic and holds him back (0-1). A ship at sail can be seen in the distance. This first, unnumbered, card of the tarot is usually called the Fool, but as the *Ship of Fools Tarot* is made up almost entirely of such characters, our card stresses the tarot Fool as traveler, pilgrim, adventurer, and vagabond. Early Italian tarot cards often show a figure resembling a beggar for this card. The *Narrenschiff* provides a beggar fool and his family that would accord well with both the early tarot

0-2, *Narrenschiff*

0-3, *Narrenschiff*

0-4, *Tarot de Marseille*

0-5, *Rider-Waite Tarot*

fool-as-beggar and the later *Tarot de Marseille* tradition of jester-as-traveler—even to the little family dog (*Von bettlern*) (0-2). But as the Vagabond card is perhaps the signature image of this tarot, the author has opted to design a more lively wandering fool from several different *Narrenschiff* sources. His pose and clothes, for example, come from a print that warns us to put out fires in our own home before we rush to fight any flames next door (0-3).

The Vagabond's bag of belongings tied to a stick and the biting dog echo the *Tarot de Marseille* tradition, in which the little dog often sinks its teeth into the fool's rump, as the hapless fellow's trousers fall around his knees (0-4). The little ship recalls the theme of the Ship of Fools, while the *Tarot de Marseille* images have only summary landscapes, if any. Landscape takes an important role in the *Waite-Smith* Fool card, as the elegantly dressed young man—not a jester at all—steps blithely very near the edge of an overhanging cliff (0-5). The cliff, never present before *Waite-Smith*, has become an expected detail. A little dog scampers alongside, to warn the fool, or to join him in a *folie à deux*. As dangerous as the situation seems, the bright sun and the Fool's serene confidence make this a hopeful, inspiring image. The traveling Fool has given rise to the modern tradition of the Fool as a voyager who strikes out bravely into the unknown. His undignified appearance hides real depths: as in Shakespeare, the Fool is often more acute and honest than anyone else. He is the Divine Fool, embodied in such mischief-making gods as Greek Dionysus (Roman Bacchus), and Pan.

Divinatory meaning: A new beginning, a fresh start. Bravery, spontaneity, impetuosity, impulsiveness, rashness. Childlike innocence, hope, and idealism. Childishness, foolishness, folly, and foolery. Honesty, frankness, guilelessness, lack of tact. To wander poor, alone, without direction—or to be free, carefree, footloose, and unencumbered.

1 — The Montebank

1 THE Montebank

1-1, *Ship of Fools Tarot*

The Montebank card, numbered 1, begins the proper sequence of the tarot. In recent centuries the figure portrayed on the card has become known as the Magician, especially as a sorcerer and sage (1-1). It is clear from early decks, however, that this figure is as much a charlatan-magician as he is a Hermetic magician, and in fact he can also be seen as a kind of merchant or vendor. His name or title has been mysterious too. His enduring name in Italian, *Bagatto*, may relate to such

1-2, *Narrenschiff*

1-3, *Tarot de Marseille*

1-4, *Rider-Waite Tarot*

Renaissance traditions as Carneval pageants or *Commedia dell'Arte* theater. *Bagatella* means a thing frivolous or of little value; *bagattino* a person of little account. *Bachetta*, on the other hand, which derives from the Latin for twig and branch, is the Italian term for a pointer and baton. Thus Bagatto, and the usual French title *Bateleur*, may refer to the Magician's small staff.

The Montebank of the *Ship of Fools Tarot* is taken from a *Narren-schiff* illustration that depicts "Ritter Peter" and "Doctor Griff," a pompous old nobleman and the wise fool who admonishes him and tweaks his ear (1-2). The *Narrenschiff* chapter, (*Von groesem ruemen**), criticizes foolish boasting. The image has been altered principally by adding a sword and coin to the tabletop, and by removing the in-scribed banners above the two men. It is unusual in the tarot to see a second figure accompany the Magician on the first trump, but not in some early Italian cards, in which an audience of two or more persons, sometimes children, attends the main character. The *Tarot of Marseille* version of the *Bateleur* or Montebank (the Italian title *Mago*, "Sorcer-er," is a modern interpolation) displays the classic type: a young man standing behind a small table who wears a large hat and wields a small baton (1-3). A knife, a cup, and other oddments lie on the table before him. Most of these elements have been carried forward to Pamela Col-man Smith's Magician card, with the exception of the broad-brimmed hat (1-4). This however seems to have been transformed into the lem-niscate, or a horizontal figure eight, symbol of eternity, which floats over the young man's head. Here the objects on the Magician's table have become emphatically those of the four suits. His clothes are those of a magus or priest; gone is the plebeian doublet of the *Tarot de Mar-seille*. His concentrated look and solid stance, his gesture toward heav-en with his small wand and accompanying gesture toward the earth, the frame of vines above him and lush flowers below—all these ele-ments promote the Magician from conjurer to soothsayer.

The tarot Bagatto may have begun history as a conjuror or vendor, but he has become, with the esoteric tarot tradition of the last two hundred years, a dignified sorcerer. The deepest truth may encompass

---

* Of Great Boasting: "Knight Peter of yore / I must grab you by the ears. / It seems to me that both of us are fools, / Even though we wear knightly spurs."

both extremes: like Hermes (Mercury), the Magician inspires wisdom, but he may also instigate trickery. Hermes, the god of communication, the inventor of writing and the alphabet, is also protector of liars. The god of eloquence is also the god of silence. This trickery is not, however, the spontaneous mischief of the Fool, but instead its opposite: calculated guile, intelligent scheming. The Magician represents mastery in the world of matter: he works miracles, apparent or actual. He does this with the objects on his table, which can be seen as the entirety of creation distilled into its four fundamental elements: air, water, fire, and earth; as represented by the signs of the four suits.

D ivinatory meaning: Mastery and skill, intelligence and ingenuity. Persuasive eloquence, Hermetic silence. Prestidigitation, sleight of hand, skilled trickery, or, conversely, magical transformation and miracle making. Practical knowledge, occult wisdom, confident fluency, concerted activity. Innovation, invention, and novelty. Science and technology, in all their triumphant promise and alarming perils.

2 — The Papess

2 THE PAPESS

2-1, *Ship of Fools Tarot*

Often now titled the High Priestess, the card originally called the Papess or Female Pope in the early Tarot follows the Magician or Montebank. In the *Ship of Fools Tarot* this card has been given to an illustration of the personification of wisdom (2-1). The only change made to the image has been to replace the woman's conventional crown with a three-tiered papal tiara. Brant's illustrators present wisdom as a version of Ecclesia, or the church personified (2-2). She stands, leaning on a cushion, in a wooden pulpit within a crowded

2-2, *Narrenschiff*

2-3, *Tarot de Marseille*

2-4, *Rider-Waite Tarot*

vaulted church. Men, women, children, and assorted fools sit on the floor or stand in the background. Wisdom, or, for our purposes, the Papess, is winged, gestures with her right hand, and holds a slender scepter surmounted by the dove of the Holy Spirit in her right. The hand of God, encircled by a halo, points to her from a cluster of small clouds. This illustration appears twice in Brant's book, for "The Teaching of Wisdom" (*Die ler der wisheit**) and "The Wise Man" (*Der wis man***). Traditional Tarot cards show the Papess as a seated female figure dressed in papal regalia. Our version of the *Marseille* Papessa is a mature woman, seated, with a book of wisdom open on her lap (2-3). A simple drapery hangs behind her. The *Waite-Smith* High Priestess has been transformed from a female pope into a pagan priestess (2-4). She too is seated in dignified robes, but her headdress and flanking columns are Egyptian.

The tarot Papess remains one of the great puzzles of the entire series. She is, after all, a frankly heretical image and idea, likely to irritate the powers-that-be. On the other hand, the legend of Pope Joan— that a woman had succeeded in hiding her sex and ascended to the throne of Saint Peter—was a standby of medieval legend. Joan was, however, more than an artifact of folklore: Vatican historians included her in the official roster of popes. Perhaps then the Papess of the tarot is Joan, or even a thirteenth-century Milanese abbess, Manfreda, who was elected papess by the heretical Guglielmites. Intriguing also is the approach proposed by Tom Tadfor Little, that the Papess is not a particular personage (as indeed none of her companions is), but instead simply the consort and female counterpart of the Pope, just as the Empress is that of the Emperor. Heretical, yes, but rather innocently so: a memory of gnosticism, or an instinctual dualism, as the Papess maintains the symmetry of her section of the trumps of the deep game of tarot.

The Papess can be seen as Sophia, the embodiment of the highest spiritual wisdom; Shekinah, the feminine radiant divine splendor; and

---

* The Teaching of Wisdom: "He who enjoys hearing and learning wisdom, / And turns to it every day, / He will be honored for eternity."

** The Wise Man: "Of fools I have said much, / So that all might be informed of their folly; / But he who is clever through and through, / Should read the words of my friend Virgil."

Anima, in Jung's fourth and highest stage. In earlier works (*A Renaissance Tarot*, U.S. Games, 1994), I have associated this card with the goddess Demeter (Ceres), patroness of Eleusis, guardian of the Earth's mysteries; but the Papess can also be seen as Athena (Minerva), goddess of the mind, progenetrix of wisdom.

Divinatory meaning: Feminine wisdom, female spirituality. Hidden traditions, ancient rites, secret heritage. Oral traditions, unwritten histories, old wives' tales, folk medicines, primordial memory. The conceptual and meditative aspect of the Anima, or the female principle, as opposed to the active and fertile Empress.

3 — The Empress

3 THE EMPRESS

3-1, *Ship of Fools Tarot*

The Empress, the third numbered trump of the tarot, is portrayed in the *Ship of Fools Tarot* by an allegorical personification of Folly itself, from an illustration for "Of the Power of Fools" (*Von der gewalt der narren**) (3-1). She is a proud monarch, seated in a festive tent decorated with a motif of Fools' caps. Crowded around, and chained to her, are worthies and dignitaries of all kinds. Anyone can be a slave

---

* Of the Power of Fools: "Folly has a vast tent / In which is encamped the entire world, / Especially those of power and money."

3-2, *Narrenschiff*

3-3, *Tarot de Marseille*

3-4, *Rider-Waite Tarot*

of Folly, the image says, including—or especially—the powerful and the proud. No detail has been changed from the *Narrenschiff* original (3-2). The Empress of the *Tarot de Marseille* sits enthroned and crowned (3-3). She holds a scepter and shield. Her throne rises behind her in two curves, a design element that with the passage of time and the misunderstanding of printers evolved sometimes into wings. The *Waite-Smith* Empress is a soft Earth goddess: no stiff pose, heavy gown, or hard-edged crown (3-4). Instead, she half reclines on pillows. A crown of blooms or stars and a flowing embroidered negligee are her dress. The scepter she holds is small; her shield, heart-shaped and inscribed with the sign of Venus, leans against her couch. Lush vegetation surrounds her.

The Empress represents the active and fruitful aspect of the female principle, in contrast to the more remote or abstract Papess. She is matronly and motherly, like Mary, the Mother of God, and like Hera (Juno), the matriarch of Olympus.

Divinatory meaning: Feminine power and fruitfulness. Fertility, abundance, generosity, motherliness, nurturing. Home and hearth. Matriarchal traditions, family life and child rearing, domestic economies. Feminine splendors: luxury, elegance, and refinements. The Empress card, if inauspiciously placed, encompasses the possibility of a smothering, overly doting protectiveness.

4 — The Emperor

4-1, *Ship of Fools Tarot*

The Emperor wears a long, fur-lined cloak and stands on a cliff above the sea (4-1). Before him a Fool seems to mock or challenge him. The ruler of kings is bearded and wears the high, conical crown of the Holy Roman Empire. The image combines elements from different *Narrenschiff* sources. The *Marseille* Emperor is usually shown seated in profile, his legs crossed (4-2). The Imperial eagle emblazons the escutcheon at his feet. The Emperor's scepter is floral and baroque. The *Waite-Smith* Emperor is shown frontally on a throne adorned with carved rams' heads (4-3). His visage is stern, his beard long and white. He holds a scepter surmounted with a cross and small circle, creating a version of the Egyptian Ankh.

Father figure and supreme ruler, the Emperor corresponds to such patriarchal gods as Zeus (Jupiter), sky god and ruler of all beings, human and divine.

Divinatory meaning: Rule, authority, executive leadership. Worldly sophistication, proud self-reliance. Government, rules, societal structures and strictures. The masculine principle expressed in its active mode: as clan leader, father figure, and man of action.

4-2, Tarot de Marseille

4-3, Rider-Waite Tarot

5 — The Pope

5 THE POPE

5-1, *Ship of Fools Tarot*

Trump number five is often called the Hierophant or High Priest, but in early days was known as the Pope, and arrayed according-ly. The Pope of the *Ship of Fools Tarot* (5-1) comes directly from Brant's *Narrenschiff*, from the woodcut illustration for chapter ninety-nine, "Of the Decline of the Faith" (*Von abgang des glouben**) (5-2). In our

---

* Of the Decline of the Faith: "I implore you all, gentlemen small and great, /
Think of the fate of the common weal, / And how it grants me alone the dunce's
cap."

5-2, *Narrenschiff*

5-3, *Tarot de Marseille*

5-4, *Rider-Waite Tarot*

card design an accompanying Emperor and a small retinue of cardinals and dignitaries have been omitted. The rest of the image, though, is as found in Brant: the Pope stands to one side, in disputatious gesture with the kneeling Fool before him, who holds out his cap and seems to be laughing. Two more young Fools chatter and observe from a high wall. In Brant the intent of the image and the chapter is to admonish and challenge the princes of Europe, ecclesiastical and secular, to address the threat to Christendom of the Ottoman Turk. The image also works more broadly as a challenge to the pride of power. The Pope of the *Tarot of Marseille* gestures with one hand and holds his bishop's crook in the other (5-3). He wears the distinctive beehive-shaped papal crown. In our example the accompanying figures in front of him, tonsured priests kneeling and seen from the rear, have been abstracted almost out of existence. Their shaved heads have become meaningless circles, their shoulders flat curves and stripes. These subsidiary figures have been restored to their human dignity in the *Waite-Smith* card, where they flank the throne of the Hierophant (5-4). The Hierophant also maintains the papal associations of the old tarot, as he wears priestly vestments. The papal tiara is on his head, his gesture of benediction and the crook in his left hand are of the standard type. Two Romanesque columns frame him.

The Pope represents official spiritual tradition—more broadly, of course, than the particular tradition of the Roman Catholic Church, of which the supreme pontiff is head.

Divinatory meaning: Spiritual traditions, organized religion. Education and systems of knowledge. Officialdom, bureaucracy, hierarchy. The masculine principle in its contemplative mode. Tradition that can be hide-bound or stultifying, but also here is the valuable wisdom of traditional culture, the advice and guidance of society's elders.

6 — Love

6 LOVE

6-1, *Ship of Fools Tarot*

The sixth trump of the tarot usually shows a pair of courting lovers. Early Tarot cards of this theme included one or more pairs of lovers, sometimes with Cupid himself presiding from a pedestal or flying overhead and aiming his bow. Our version of this card shows Venus herself, in an image taken in its entirety from Brant's book (6-1, 2). She is a tall, elegantly dressed young woman with a great mass of hair. Her left hand is raised benevolently, her right hand holds the ends of ropes that bind two fools, a friar, a seated monkey, a standing

6-2, *Narrenschiff*

6-3, *Tarot de Marseille*

6-4, *Rider-Waite Tarot*

donkey, and even her own blindfolded child, Eros (Cupid), who points his bow and arrow aimlessly. A magnificent pair of wings rise from Venus' shoulders, and from the shelter of one wing peeks a skeleton, the figure of Death. The scene takes place in a city street. Brant's text and illustration for the chapter "Of Foolish Amours" (*Von boulschafft**) show the power of Love, Venus, as an all-powerful tyrant in her seductive power to make fools of men and animals. From the *Tarot of Marseille* comes the later tarot tradition of a male figure flanked by two female ones, as if he were faced with the choice between the two, or as if the crowned woman were blessing the young couple (6-3). Here, too, Cupid presides, flying and aiming his bow, from above. Another transformation came with the solution provided for the *Waite-Smith* series (6-4). Here Cupid has been turned into a solemn archangel AND the two lovers have been transposed to Eve and Adam.

The goddess of love, personified in Aphrodite (Venus), binds us all to her in a way similar to that which binds us to the Empress: with cords and leashes. The bonds of Brant's Empress Folly are especially those of wealth and power; those of Venus are of love and passion. A failing to be satirized for Brant, but a necessary and joyous reality for humanity: the bonds of love are the very stuff of life. Romantic love is a sweet bondage, as so many poets have told us. Other bonds of love, though, are just as important: those of family, of friendship, of community.

Divinatory meanings: Love, romance, passion, attraction, courtship, marriage, alliance, friendship, fellow feeling, companionship. Sometimes blind love, impetuous, infatuation, obsessive passion, base lust. Love, though, makes the world go round, even if it also often makes fools of us.

---

* Of Foolish Amours: "To my line I have hitched many a fool, / Monkey, mule, and love-loon, / Whom I seduce, betray, and deceive."

7 — The Cart

7-1, *Ship of Fools Tarot*

The seventh numbered trump of the Tarot is almost always called the Chariot, but a humbler term, the cart, has been used for the *Ship of Fools Tarot* (7-1). In fact there is often no distinction between the two terms in medieval languages; the more rustic word suits the unpolished reality of the *Ship of Fools Tarot*. The image is taken directly from a *Narrenschiff* title page, where it is combined with another image of Fools thronging a sea-borne ship (7-2). Brant's wagon then is full of fools on their way to the fleets that will carry them to far-off

7-2, *Narrenschiff*

7-3, *Tarot de Marseille*

7-4, *Rider-Waite Tarot*

Narragonia, a fictional land of folly. (The name Narragonia jokingly fuses the word for Fool, Narr, with the name of the Iberian region, Aragon.)

Early Chariot cards vary in imagery between a celebratory female figure and a martial male one. The second type became standard with the *Tarot de Marseille* (7-3). Always shown frontally, with two small horses naively foreshortened, the *Marseille* Chariot carries a proud princely warrior in full armor. The *Waite-Smith* image takes up this type, but replaces the horses with couching Egyptian sphinxes, one black and one white (7-4). Early tarot cards never show a contrast of this kind between the Chariot's two animals, of dark animal paired with pale. This innovation can suggest Plato's metaphor from the Symposium of the well-favored and ill-favored horses: the competing forces that pull the chariot of the human soul toward virtue or vice. The dark beast paired with the light also echoes the dualistic imagery that runs through the tarot, and that informs all life: night and day, Moon and Sun, male and female. The closest classical parallel to the male charioteer of the later tarot tradition is Ares (Mars), the god of war. The earlier tarot Chariot cards find a different classical parallel in Nike, winged goddess of victory, who presides with her leafy crown from a ceremonial chariot. The rustic Cart of the *Ship of Fools Tarot* has many charioteers and a single donkey to pull it. They have some of Roman Mars' exultancy, none of his terrible dignity.

Divinatory meaning: Movement, progress, getting ahead, moving forward. Victory parade, triumphal chariot. Triumph, rolling over one's enemies, crushing the opposition, overcoming obstacles. Reckless progress, unruly advancement.

8 — *Justice*

8 JUSTICE

8-1, *Ship of Fools Tarot*

Justice is the eighth Trump in the traditional tarot, although she often trades places with Strength in position number eleven in the esoteric tarot of recent generations. Our Justice comes directly and completely from Brant, where a standing fool (8-1) blindfolds the familiar figure of Justice. Justice, a young woman with flowing hair, holds an enormous balance and scales in one hand and a sword in the other. These are, of course, her customary attributes to this day. Even

8-2, *Narrenschiff*

8-3, *Tarot de Marseille*

8-4, *Rider-Waite Tarot*

her blindfold is standard (though less often seen in the tarot), for Justice is understood to be blind in the sense that she is unbiased and impartial. In our case, however, the fool renders Justice blind in the sense of depriving her of her rightful role. Brant's chapter seventy-one is titled "Quarreling and Going to Court" (*Zancken vnd zu gericht gon**) (8-2). It describes the folly of those who recklessly take their every dispute before a judge.

Justice sits on a throne and holds her attributes in most traditional versions of the card, including the *Tarot of Marseille* (8-3). Her throne, like that of the Empress, was misunderstood by some cardmakers over time and transformed into wings. Pamela Colman Smith's Justice follows the accepted tradition, but gains an increased naturalism (8-4). The young female personification wears a flowing robes and a simple crown. A curtain hangs between two columns behind her seat.

For the ancient Greeks, Justice was sometimes Themis, the only Titaness permitted to remain on Mount Olympus after the coup in heaven of Zeus and his siblings. It was wise, even necessary, to stay her banishment. Dike, a daughter of Themis by Zeus, also embodied justice. Justice remains today a vital part of life: for the individual who hopes for fairness in dealings small and large; and for the community that must strive to maintain the principles of justice or sink into brutality and tyranny.

D ivinatory meaning: Justice, fairness, vindication, just outcome. Reckoning, decision, judgment. Reason, wisdom, sound judgment. Social peace, the rule of law, societal order. Perspective and even-handedness in relationships. Our card also warns that Justice should be tempered with mercy; it should be impartial but not arbitrary. And Justice should not be exploited or manipulated.

---

* Quarreling and Going to Court: "He will soon be panting, he who / Constantly bickers like a child, / And thinks that he can blind the truth."

9 — *The Hermit*

9 THE HERMIT

9-1, *Ship of Fools Tarot*

The ninth Trump of the Tarot is known nowadays as the Hermit, a title that derives from the tradition of the *Tarot de Marseille*. The Hermit card usually shows an old man, dressed rather like a monk, who leans on a cane and who carries a lamp. Earlier versions of the card, however, show a figure that represents Old Age or Time personified, in the person of the god Saturn. The *Ship of Fools Tarot* image is adapted from an illustration in Brant that reminds the young to

9-2, *Narrenschiff*

9-3, *Narrenschiff*

9-4, *Tarot de Marseille*

9-5, *Rider-Waite Tarot*

honor their parents (*Ere vatter und mutter**) (9-1, 2). This figure lacks the lamp familiar from the *Marseille* tradition, but otherwise resembles the traditional type, with his long robes and cane. His fool's cap places him apart from the usual Hermit, as does the accompanying fool who challenges him with an insulting gesture.

Another *Narrenschiff* image, that "Of Old Fools" (*Von alten narren***), could also be used quite unchanged for this trump (9-3). This is a bitterly funny image of a miserable old man with one foot literally in the grave. He struggles forward on two canes. Death has veritably "hooked" the old man already; the Grim Reaper's scythe is planted in the old man's buttocks. Death will yank the old man to his reward at any moment, as a fisherman tugs a hooked fish—yet the old fool persists in his folly. The author has chosen however to assemble a different image, because the *Narrenschiff* Old Fool image, as a tarot trump, would lack both the elements that dignify him as Kronos or Saturn in early Italian tarots, and the itinerant, monkish attributes of the Hermit. The *Marseille* and *Waite-Smith* cards show the latter type: a bearded old man, seen in profile, holds up a lamp (an hourglass in early cards) and leans on a walking stick (9-4, 5). His dress is a hooded monk's robe. Pamela Colman Smith followed the iconography of the *Marseille* exactly, but she created a more striking and elegant image by showing the Hermit in a tall, slender, standing profile. The Hermit's lantern gains prominence, held high before him—although the bearded figure seems to be looking inward rather than where his light leads.

A young fool, the outward projection of his inward folly, besets the Hermit of the *Ship of Fools.* The Hermit too is a fool, as his fool's cap shows. Brant, we can imagine, would warn against the error of the pride possible in seeking humility too earnestly; or of the possible foolishness inherent in the solitary life, for the hermit's life doesn't bring automatic wisdom. But the Hermit's example remains a vital one. He shows us the power of the quiet inward spiritual journey. He

---

*   Honor thy Father and Mother: "Always honor father and mother / That God may grant you long life / And lay no shame on upon you."

** Of Old Fools: "Even with one foot in the grave / And the flaying knife up my ass / Yet will I not forsake my foolishness."

demonstrates the advantages of solitude, reflection, and meditation. Among the gods a parallel can be seen in the Roman Saturn, ruler of the mythical golden age, but also a deposed and solitary figure. The legendary philosopher Diogenes, who searches with his lamp of truth for a single, truly honest man, also provides a parallel for the Hermit. Saturnine bitterness is an inherent danger of the Hermit, for his solitude can become misanthropy.

Divinatory meaning: Spiritual search, solitary searching, meditation, reflection. Solitude, philosophical quest, inward journey. The quest for truth. Consciousness of the passage of time, of the inevitability of change. Accidia, or Saturnine stasis and sadness, may accompany the Hermit, but his is also the dignity of wisdom and experience. No fool is worse than an old fool. The Hermit also reminds us to embrace wisdom as we age.

10 — The Wheel of Fortune

10 THE WHEEL OF FORTUNE

10-1, *Ship of Fools Tarot*

The tenth Trump comes unchanged from Brant's book and resembles countless versions of this theme from every period (10-1, 2). Fortune herself, the personification of chance and opportunity, is not present in this image—or indeed in most versions of the tarot card. Instead the wheel itself takes center stage, while around it spin lucky or hapless humans and creatures. As often occurs in the tarot, in Brant these figures are a combination of human and animal: a donkey-headed fool, like Shakespeare's Bottom, rises on the wheel's right;

10-2, *Narrenschiff*

10-3, *Tarot de Marseille*

10-4, *Rider-Waite Tarot*

another ass presides from the summit of the wheel. A third figure, a fool who is a donkey below the waist, is falling from the wheel's height. Two details set apart the Brant image from the usual tarot image: a tomb-like ditch opens up below the unlucky falling fool, and the handle of the wheel is turned by a cord descending from the hand of Heaven. The image is used twice in Brant, for "Of Happenstance" (*Von gluckes fall**), where we are warned of changes in fortune, and in "Of the End of Power" (*Von end des gewalltes*), which recounts how many of the mighty have fallen. The *Tarot de Marseille* image, with its hybrid animal creatures spinning around a wheel, perfectly accords with the *Narrenschiff* print (10-3). The *Waite-Smith* version has been rendered mystical (10-4). The Wheel is now a dial inscribed with magical letters and symbols; the animals around it are mythological and Egyptian. Clouds billow all around the floating disk. The Tetramorph, the four symbols of the Evangelists found traditionally in the tarot only on the World card, complete the design.

The Wheel of Fortune, in the tarot and in European tradition in general, has long symbolized the role of chance in life. Seemingly without rhyme or reason, we can be thrown high into the lap of luxury, or cast down into penury. In love, in health, in every possible way, we can find ourselves stunned by good fortune or ill. Brant warns us, as would every other medieval or Renaissance writer, to be humble in good fortune and patient in times of trouble, for the Wheel may turn again and cast us down, or up. Fortune with her wheel descends from the writings of the late antique Roman philosopher Boethius. In earlier classical thought, Fortuna was portrayed with a ship's rudder, for she turns this way and that; or with a cornucopia, because her favor brings abundance. In this favorable aspect she is called Fortuna Bona, and is sometimes shown with wings.

---

* Of Happenstance: "He who sits high on the wheel of fortune / Waits only to fall, hurt, / And take an inevitable bath."

Divinatory meaning: Change in fortune, the role of chance in life, sudden shift in luck. Coincidences and synchronicity. An opportunity, perhaps a fleeting one. The possibility of reversals and setbacks. Cycles, in time and in events. An admonition to enjoy, humbly, our moments of good fortune, and to endure difficult times with patience and hope.

11 — Strength

11 STRENGTH

11-1, *Ship of Fools Tarot*

The Strength card, number eleven in the traditional sequence, is adapted for the *Ship of Fools Tarot* from an illustration in Brant that lampoons recklessness (*Von vnbesinten narren**) (11-1). The donkey and the fool are seen in an open landscape that includes a fanciful hill town. The only change in the image is that the fool now seizes his

---

* Of Careless Fools: "He who rides before tightening the saddle belt / And does not betake himself in good time / Is worthy of scorn as he falls to one side."

11-2, *Narrenschiff*

11-3, *Tarot de Marseille*

11-4, *Rider-Waite Tarot*

mount by the mouth rather than by the mane (11-2). In this way the image echoes a traditional version of the tarot card, that of a female personification of Strength who wrestles with the lion, or gently opens its mouth. This image in turn is a curious hybrid of more common versions of the virtue Fortitude, which is customarily shown either as a calm female figure holding a column, or the more animated "exemplum" of Hercules struggling with the lion. The *Marseille* Strength card demonstrates the former type (11-3). The *Waite-Smith* Strength card softens and intellectualizes the theme: Strength is no longer a female warrior but now a serene goddess who gently grasps the jaws of an equally calm lion (11-4). The broad-brimmed hat of the *Marseille* maiden has been changed, as has the similar hat of the Magician, into a floating horizontal figure eight, or lemniscate, symbol of eternity.

Three of the four cardinal virtues appear among the tarot trumps: Justice, Temperance, and Strength (the fourth, Prudence, doesn't—a perennial puzzle). The virtues are more than personifications of admirable qualities. They are, in the worldview of the middle ages, the essential four pillars that sustain any and all moral success, in an individual or a society. Strength then is not a neutral quality, mere physical or mental forcefulness, but instead Fortitude, the quality of heroes and saints. The emblematic hero of the ancients, Herakles (Hercules), best embodies the tarot Strength card. In fact, one of the earliest known versions of the card, from the *Visconti-Sforza* pack, portrays the Strength card as Hercules himself in the act of bludgeoning a miniature Nemean lion.

The *Ship of Fools* card shows a very different character. Rather than a noble female personification gently subduing a lion, or a heroic Herakles wrestling with the beast, instead fool grabs his donkey by the jaws, while sprawled on the animal's back.

Divinatory meaning: Strength, fortitude, patience, self-control. Nobility of mind, moral strength. If excessive or misguided, the card may signal stubbornness or moral rigidity, but firm moral resolve and unwavering courage are its usual gifts. The Strength card also suggests the kind of balance represented by the maiden and the lion: the opposites and complements of the cerebral and the physical; the tame and the wild; the human and the natural. A reminder to prepare the mind and body for action: latch properly your donkey's saddle; remember to buckle your seatbelt.

12 — The Hanged Man

12 THE HANGED MAN

12-1, *Ship of Fools Tarot*

The Hanged Man, trump number eleven, is adapted closely from the illustration of Brant's chastisement of vaunting self-reliance (*Von eygenrichtigkeit**), chapter thirty-six of the *Narrenschiff* (12-1, 2). For Brant this is the foolishness of one who recklessly reaches for the too-high bird's nest. For the tarot image, a cord attaching the

---

*   Of Self-Endeavor: "He who tries to fly by his own power, / And to climb to the
     nests on high, / Will often find himself lying on the ground."

12-2, *Narrenschiff*

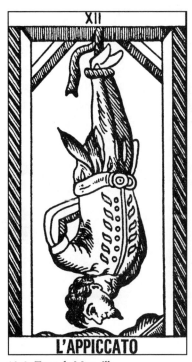

12-3, *Tarot de Marseille*

12-4, *Rider-Waite Tarot*

fool's ankle to a tree branch creates an emblem similar to the traditional Hanged Man.

The *Marseille* card shows the traditional tarot type, although in this particular case the unfortunate man hangs from both ankles (12-3). The *Waite-Smith* Hanged Man presents the more familiar pose, with one leg crossed behind a straight leg (12-4). Nontraditional, however, is the Hanged Man's halo. The earliest records in fact give this trump titles such as *Il Traditore*, or "the Traitor." Certain early Italian cards portray him holding one or two spilling moneybags, apparent references to the greatest traitor of Christian tradition, Judas Iscariot. The esoteric tarot tradition, however, has always understood the Hanged Man to be a kind of martyr or saint.

Prometheus provides an analogy from classical mythology to the noble self-sacrifice of the Hanged Man. Prometheus brought the gift of fire to humankind, against the express orders of the king of the gods. For this he submitted, knowingly, to a terrible punishment. The *Ship of Fools* Hanged Man is no Prometheus, but he too has brought his punishment on himself. In undergoing his trial he changes, grows, and learns.

Divinatory meaning: Sacrifice, suspension, stasis, delay, being stuck. A period of trial, perhaps self-imposed, that can lead to wisdom and fulfillment. The Hanged Man can represent the danger of a mistaken impulse to martyrdom, of taking on unnecessary tribulation.

13 — Death

13 DEATH

13-1, *Ship of Fools Tarot*

The Death card always occupies the thirteenth place in the tarot trump sequence. Death, alone among the trumps, is sometimes numbered but often not named, as if it might be inauspicious to label him. Our tarot card is taken unchanged from Brant's chapter eighty-five, "On Not Providing for Death" (*Nit fursehen den dot**) (13-1, 2).

---

* On Not Providing for Death: "O Death, may nobility, wealth, strength, or youth / Have peace and quiet of you? / All that which has found life / And yet is mortal, must surely perish."

13-2, *Narrenschiff*

13-3, *Tarot de Marseille*

13-4, *Rider-Waite Tarot*

The scene shows a shocked fool accosted by the skeletal figure of Death. The fool holds a sort of bouquet of little bells; Death hoists the fool's coffin. "*Du Blibst*," Death says, "you stay." Early tarot cards show Death on horseback, or standing with scythe in hand, as in our version of the *Tarot de Marseille* (13-3). Death here is portrayed in the act of harvesting lives in a field where heads and hands lie alongside small plants. Death is a knight in black armor on a white horse in the *Waite-Smith* card (13-4). The skeletal knight holds the reins of his mount and a large black flag adorned with a heraldic rose. In Death's path are three figures: a supplicating bishop, a swooning woman, and a kneeling child. The Sun sets in the distance, framed by two small towers.

The Death card understandably alarms at first glance. Death is all around us, all the time, and each of us will end our lives in death. However, the card does not announce, necessarily, anything like literal death. Instead the end of a certain situation, a moment of transformation, may be the real meaning of the card in a reading. In order to begin anything anew, to start fresh, a prevailing situation must die and come to an end.

D ivinatory meaning: Ending, resolution, transformation, finality. Also rebirth and metamorphosis.

14 — Temperance

14-1, *Ship of Fools Tarot*

$\mathbb{T}$here is no figure similar to the traditional image of the virtue Temperance among the illustrations for Brant's book. Therefore an original treatment of Temperance (14-1), a standing fool who pours the contents of one jug of liquid into another, has been created from diverse elements of the *Narrenschiff*. The pitchers overflow, watering a flower growing between the fool's feet. Temperance, as portrayed in the tarot, is properly female, and she does not spill her water and wine, for she tempers them instead within her containers, as she tempers extremes in the individual soul. The *Marseille* card depicts this type: Temperance stands, swaying gracefully (14-2). She pours one pitcher's contents into another. She also has wings, a customary attribute for her now, but not always present in early renderings of the tarot Virtue—or, for that matter, of the many versions of Temperance that can be found in the ambient European culture of the middle ages and Renaissance. The *Waite-Smith* Temperance shares all the *Marseille* symbols, with adjustments (14-3). The pitchers have become chalices; the rather androgynous figure stands straight; her head is encircled by a halo. The landscape in the *Smith* image includes important new details: a pond or lake in the foreground in which the angelic figure dips one foot; a stand of nearby irises; a glowing sun that crowns a distant mountain-top, at the end of a long road. Temperance classically mixes her water and wine—or milk and honey—within her two vessels; our foolish Temperance is spilling some of his liquid gifts. This waywardness has a happy result, as the pitchers nourish the little flower at his feet.

14-2, *Tarot de Marseille*

14-3, *Rider-Waite Tarot*

Divinatory meaning: Harmonious blending, sweet admixture, spiritual balance. Tempering one tendency with its opposite or complement. Androgyny. Grace, poise, moderation, nothing in excess. If reversed or otherwise ill favored, the card may represent alienation or polarization, aN inclination to imbalance.

15 — The Devil

15 THE DEVIL

15-1, *Ship of Fools Tarot*

The image for the *Ship of Fools* Devil card comes directly from Brant's book, where it illustrates chapter twenty, which discusses found treasure (*Von schatz fynden**) (15-1, 2). Here a fool strains on his leash toward a cache of discovered loot, heedless of the danger to his soul in keeping ill-gotten gains, unconcerned at his bondage to the

---

* Of Finding Treasure: "He who finds something, and takes it as his, / And believes that God intends it to be so: / He has been shat upon by the Devil."

15-2, *Narrenschiff*

15-3, *Tarot de Marseille*

15-4, *Rider-Waite Tarot*

Devil. The *Tarot de Marseille* Devil is a monster that stands on a small plinth to which are chained two captive imps (15-3). The Devil and his captives are furry beasts that stand upright. The Devil, himself, has large leathery wings and horns on his head. The *Waite-Smith* follows the *Marseille* precedent in most particulars (15-4). Here, though, the Devil's scepter is a flaming club, held downward. The greatest difference with the earlier card is the transformation of the small captive demons into attractive human nudes. These characters remain devils, with their horns and tails, and they too are chained to their master's pedestal, but in their attractive humanity they are transposed portraits of the Eve and Adam of the *Waite-Smith* card of the Lovers. The *Waite* Devil himself, though, remains grotesque and buffoonish with his grimacing goat's head, fleshy upper body, furry satyr's legs, clawed feet, and bat's wings.

The Devil, as expected, represents evil and temptation. For Brant and his time, the Devil was a terrible, living presence. For Brant, obedience to religious and state authority provide the best defense against him. Evil—cruelty, brutality, selfishness—remains an appalling a part of our own time, even if one doesn't take the Devil seriously as an individual personage or manifest force. Another face of the medieval Devil—and the tarot Devil—is his primal, pagan one. For the Devil is also Pan, or Priapus: gods of wild nature, of amoral (not immoral) pleasure, of fertile abandon. Pan relentlessly accosts every nymph and shepherd boy, causes panic in the unwary traveler, but there is joy too in his rustic appetites. Priapus protects orchards and gardens, threatening thieves with his enormous, always-erect phallus. The Hebrews and then the Christians reviled such excess, and gave their idea of the Devil the physical trappings of the pagan gods of fertility.

Divinatory meaning: Wickedness, temptation, immorality, evil, cruelty. Excess, self-indulgence, debauchery.

16 — The Tower

16-1, *Ship of Fools Tarot*

The Tower card shows a half-timbered house engulfed by flames and a fool who has thrust his head apprehensively from an upstairs window. House and head are about to be struck by the hammer of heaven, wielded by a hand emerging from a mass of cloud and flame (16-1). This image comes directly from Brant, except that the houses and street scene on the right side of the image have been replaced with an open landscape, to isolate the house and render it more like a traditional tarot image (16-2). The established imagery of

16-2, *Narrenschiff*

16-3, *Tarot de Marseille*

16-4, *Rider-Waite Tarot*

the card usually includes an image of a tower, struck by lightning, from which one or two unhappy victims fall. Brant's illustration accompanies the verses that warn of "vaunting luck" (*Von veberhe-bung glucks**), warning that hubris and complacency will be punished with misfortune. This is precisely the traditional meaning given to the Tarot image. Both the *Tarot de Marseille* and the *Waite-Smith* series demonstrate this (16-3, 4). The *Marseille* tower is struck by a lightning bolt. A great crown topples from the summit of the building; two men fall to earth. Small circles rain down from heaven. The *Waite-Smith* is almost identical in iconography, although the little circles are now small flames, and the tower stands on a mountaintop rather than on a plain.

The Tower announces a dramatic change of fortune, often in catastrophic guise. Here then is perhaps the most inauspicious of the tarot trumps; more fearsome, for example, than the Death card, but sudden dislocation is a part of every life, and it is also true that many good things are born from failure or disaster. These beneficial results may only show themselves with time, though, for when misfortune strikes it can be difficult indeed to foresee any happy outcome.

Divinatory meaning: Debacle, adversity, distress, calamity. Hubris punished, pride taking a fall; but also the hardships visited on the innocent. Cleansing setback, clearing the decks, fires that will foster new growth. Clearing the decks, an opportunity for new beginnings. Surprise, the unexpected. Acts of God, *force majeure*, dramatic acts of nature.

---

*   Of Vaunting Luck: "He who believes that he is blessed in everything, / And who feels that luck will never leave him, / He surely will feel fate's cudgel in the end."

17 — The Stars

17-1, *Ship of Fools Tarot*

The Stars is trump seventeen (17-1, 2). This card is titled in the plural in Italian tarots, in the singular in French and English ones. As the *Ship of Fools* reflects as much as possible the early tarot, the plural is used here. Most recent decks include a Star card that shows a nude star maiden, kneeling at water's edge with a pitcher of pouring water, as in our *Marseille* and *Waite-Smith* illustrations (17-3, 4). The oldest Italian cards, though, have any number of different images on the card, often precisely like that chosen for the *Ship of Fools Tarot.*

17-2, *Narrenschiff*

17-3, *Tarot de Marseille*

17-4, *Rider-Waite Tarot*

The corresponding image from Brant's book is exactly as seen here, except the Sun and the Moon, present in the original, have been removed to avoid confusion with the cards that follow. The intention of Brant in the chapter "Of Astrology" (*Von achtung des gstirns**) is, as always, a moralizing one: to admonish the reader to ignore astrological and other superstitions.

The Star cards of the *Tarot de Marseille* and *Waite-Smith* decks closely resemble each other. Both have an eight-pointed star at the top center, encircled by other smaller stars, and a nude maiden kneeling on one knee below. Even the charming minor detail of a bird perched atop a small distant tree appears in both images. The star maiden pours out the contents of two pitchers. The *Waite-Smith* image makes clear that the water from one pitcher is pouring into a lake, as one foot of the young woman rests in the water. The other knee and the contents of the second pitcher make contact with the solid ground. As is often the case, the version drawn by Pixie Smith differs from the *Marseille* source principally in its greater attractiveness and sophistication.

The traditional meaning of trump seventeen, as the graceful maidens would imply, is of healing, blessing, and hope. The *Ship of Fools* image differs greatly (but resembles, as has been said, some of the earliest tarot images), but the vault of stars in the night sky has always brought humankind hope and a sense of awe. Violating then the intention of Sebastian Brant, we can see the young man and the gesturing fools as beacons of hope, as they look up to a heaven sprinkled with stars and crossed by flitting birds.

Divinatory meaning: Hope, healing, blessing, benediction. Tranquility, repose, and peace. The favor of the heavens. Conversely, the card may warn of unrealistic hopes, superstition, and gullibility. But the Star card embodies some of the most favorable qualities represented in the Tarot.

---

* Of Astrology: "There is much superstition afoot, / Whereby men prophesy the future from the stars. / Fools all, who would pursue this nonsense."

18 — The Moon

18-1, *Ship of Fools Tarot*

he trump of the Moon shows, in the *Ship of Fools Tarot*, a fool in the act of measuring the cosmos with a compass (18-1). He looks over his shoulder at another fool; a crescent Moon hangs in the sky above. Our tarot card design follows Brant's book illustration closely for "On the Exploration of All Lands" (*Von erfarung aller land**),

---

* On the Exploration of All Lands: "He who measures heaven, earth, and sea, / Hoping thereby to secure fame, joy, and knowledge, / Must take care, lest he become a fool."

18-2, *Narrenschiff*

18-3, *Tarot de Marseille*

18-4, *Rider-Waite Tarot*

except for the inclusion of the Moon itself (18-2). The image accords with certain early Moon cards in which an astronomer-astrologer holds a compass and studies the heavens. For Brant it is folly to pursue the measurement of land and sea while neglecting to take the measure of one's own soul. Other early tarot Moon cards have a standing lunar goddess, or a simple emblem of the Moon itself. Most tarot images now descend, however, from the *Tarot de Marseille* formula: a landscape of water and distant twin towers, inhabited by a pair of dogs or wolves and a lobster-like creature rising toward land (18-3). A Moon, inscribed with a crescent and a face, hangs in the heavens. Drops of flame drop from the sky. The *Waite* image card follows the *Marseille* symbolism closely. The Moon's human profile has a pensive intensity; a long road wends into the mountainous distance (18-4).

More brilliant than the Stars, less bright than the Sun, the Moon card holds its place in the hierarchy of increasing power of the tarot trumps. With the Sun card it extends into the macrocosm the duality of yin and yang that has appeared in such cards as the Papess and Pope, Empress and Emperor. The Moon thus embodies the yin or feminine half of creation, and the feminine half of time, the night. The preeminent Moon goddess of ancient Greece and Rome was Artemis (Diana). The twin sister of Apollo, Artemis is goddess of the hunt and protectress of women, especially young girls and old women. Selene was another version of the lunar goddess, and terrifying Hecate also rules the night. Medieval philosophers condemned the Moon as the mistress of imperfect matter and flawed mortal creatures, for she presides over our "sublunar" world, below the higher and purer substances. Renaissance poets slighted the Moon, and womanhood in general, as "changeable," susceptible to phases and whims. The Moon card has similarly suffered; it was long considered a harbinger of deception and hidden dangers. This, however, has gradually changed, and the Moon is now appreciated as the brilliant queen of the night.

Divinatory meaning: The powers of the night, of the feminine side of creation. Dreams, intuition, imagination—even illusion—are forces ruled by the Moon. We can try to measure her dimensions and record her cycles but she will continue to take us off guard.

19 — The Sun

19-1, *Ship of Fools Tarot*

The Sun card of the *Ship of Fools Tarot* is taken directly from the illustration for chapter twenty-eight of the *Narrenschiff*, "Of Speaking Against God" (*Von wider gott reden**), where the fool is mocked who would compete with the Sun by building a fire in daytime (19-1, 2). This image differs from all early Sun cards of the tarot,

---

* Of Speaking Against God: "Should God carry out our will / We would be worse off in every way; / We would cry more than smile."

19-2, *Narrenschiff*

19-3, *Tarot de Marseille*

19-4, *Rider-Waite Tarot*

and from the standard pair of children found on cards from the *Tarot de Marseille* onward. In fact the earliest Sun cards range wildly in imagery, the only common element being the presence of the image of the Sun, universal symbol of power and life. A flying cherub holding up the Sun; a standing woman twisting thread; Diogenes asking Alexander to stand aside: these are among the earliest extant Sun card motifs. Two children capering in front of a low wall, under a smiling Sun, became the most common version of the card with the *Tarot de Marseille* (19-3). The *Waite-Smith* series departs from this with its naked child on horseback, its sunflowers, and its flowing banner (19-4). The low wall remains, and the great Sun above.

Divinatory meaning: The Sun card brings happiness, glory, and rejoicing. Brilliance and clarity comes with the sun. It would be foolish, of course, to attempt to compete with the brilliance of the Sun, and equally silly to "assist" the Sun by lighting signal fires in day-time. The Sun can scorch or blind, if we are foolish or unlucky, but warmth, ease, and life itself are its gifts.

20 — Judgment

20-1, *Ship of Fools Tarot*

The penultimate trump of the tarot is known as the Last Judgment, or Judgment (20-1). Once again the image for the *Ship of Fools Tarot* comes unchanged from the *Narrenschiff*, in this case from the illustration for chapter eighty-eight, called "Of Plagues and Divine Retribution" (*Von plag vnd strof gots**) (20-2). In this woodcut a lone

---

*   Of Plagues and Divine Retribution: "He who feels that God punishes too oft, / And plagues us with will and malice, / From him the plague is less than a quarter-mile distant.

20-2, *Narrenschiff*

20-3, *Tarot de Marseille*

20-4, *Rider-Waite Tarot*

fool gestures in consternation as a plague of locusts and frogs is sent down on him from Heaven. Moses and Samuel look on from heaven, unmoved by the fool's pleas for mercy. Moses wears the horns ascribed to him by medieval tradition, derived from a misreading of the Hebrew word for "rays." The image differs of course from the tarot standard, in which three or more nude figures rise rejoicing from their graves, while an angel trumpets the end of time from heaven. The standard composition appears in both the *Tarot de Marseille* and *Waite-Smith* cards (20-3, 4).

Judgment stands apart from the other tarot cards as the only expressly religious design of the series. The Last Judgment is a prominent idea and image in Christian tradition; it is the moment of resurrection and judgment portrayed in such depictions as Michelangelo's Sistine fresco. In the game of tarot this may have been merely a marker for the second-highest trump, although this hardly deprives the scene of its potency. The *Narrenschiff* image resembles the tarot trump, but also differs dramatically. The resurrected souls of the traditional tarot image rise rejoicing, and blessed; while the ill-starred fool of the *Narrenschiff* receives an undignified punishment of frogs and locusts, like the plagues sent against pharaoh.

D ivinatory meaning: Awakening, rebirth, and resurrection. Culmination, transformation, and metamorphosis. Critical mass; paradigm shift. All the birds coming home to roost, it never rains but it pours. The card can, at times, signal a moment of truth, or a time of judgment, but it usually betokens a fresh start, a new beginning, and a return to one's true nature.

21 — The World

21-1, *Ship of Fools Tarot*

The last and highest trump of the *Ship of Fools Tarot* shows a fool burdened with the weight of a great circle or disk, which encloses a landscape of mountains, waters, and houses (21-1). This disk is the world itself, rendering the fool a version of Atlas, the mythological Titan who holds up the heavens. Once again the image has been taken in its entirety from the *Narrenschiff*, from the chapter "Of Excessive

21-2, *Narrenschiff*

21-3, *Tarot de Marseille*

21-4, *Rider-Waite Tarot*

Worry" (*Von zu vil sorg**), where Sebastian Brant mocks the fool who takes on worries and responsibilities beyond his duty or capability (21-2). The earliest versions of the tarot World card vary greatly, with here a nymph and there a Mercury or Cupid; but they all include a human figure standing on, or holding up, a world-disk.

The *Tarot de Marseille* and its descendants like the *Waite-Smith* contain World cards on which a nude maiden represents the world soul (21-3, 4). She usually seems to float and dance within an oval garland that is in turn bordered on four sides by a winged man, a winged lion, a winged bull, and an eagle. These are the signs of the four Evangelists, the writers of the first four books of the New Testament: Matthew, Mark, Luke, and John. These symbols, the Tetramorph, have additional resonance: they comprise also the astrological Cross of Matter. The central or "fixed" months of each season— Aquarius, Taurus, Leo, and Scorpio (which could be represented by an eagle or sparrow hawk)—together represent the solid structure of the universe, its four corners and directions. The overall design of a human figure floating in an oval wreath surrounded by the four creatures, has another, irresistible, echo, for this is also the iconography of Christ Pantokrator, creator and ruler of the universe. It seems then that Christ, standing in his celestial lozenge or mandola, surrounded by his Evangelists, somehow became, in the enigmatic tradition of tarot symbolism, a goddess floating in her oval wreath.

The dancing maiden lends the World card an auspicious joyfulness, in marked contrast to the put-upon character. The goddess of the traditional tarot can be seen as Gaia, embodiment of the Earth itself, the embodiment of the fruitful universe.

Divinatory meaning: Attainment, completion, accomplishment, fulfillment. Spiritual integration, being in harmony within oneself and with the world. Nature in balance. This happy state can be imagined as a dancing world goddess, or as a fool, a jester Atlas, burdened with too much of a good thing.

---

* Of Excessive Worry: "He who would carry the weight of the world, / Without thinking of his own worth and troubles, / Will surely bathe in sorrow."

MINOR ARCANA

22 — Ace of Swords

22-1, *Ship of Fools Tarot*

Two fools reach out and hold on to the edges of an outsize sword planted in the ground on the *Ship of Fools* Ace of Swords (22-1). There is no single source from the *Narrenschiff* for this image; instead different illustrations provided elements. The design of the Ace of Swords of the *Tarot de Marseille* includes a prominent sword held up by a disembodied hand (22-2). Boughs of palm (or laurel) and olive cross and drape themselves around the sword and through a floating crown. Pamela Colman Smith included all these elements in the ace of the *Waite-Smith* Tarot (22-3). The *Ship of Fools* ace departs then from the usual design, but shares the central element of a monumental single sword. The two fools may be cooperating in erecting the sword, or perhaps are competing for its ownership. The aces concentrate and unify the characteristics of their suits; the Ace of Swords distills intensity and passion, pride and will.

This writer has always associated the suit of Swords with Fire, and thus with the medieval Choleric temperament, and conversely Staves with Air, the Sanguine. I am not the only tarot writer or designer to have done so, but even so this contradicts the customary association of Swords with Air and Staves (or Wands) with Fire. This latter correspondence derives from the teachings of the nineteenth-century occult society of the Golden Dawn, the source of much of our esoteric tarot tradition. Without renouncing my still firm preference for Swords-Fire, I propose to sidestep the question here by describing the feisty, even violent, character of the suit of Swords—which accords

22-2, Tarot de Marseille

22-3, Rider-Waite Tarot

perfectly with tarot tradition—without referring to Fire or Air. In this way the reader is welcome to choose the elemental correspondence that she or he prefers. For a more detailed explanation of my preference for the association of Swords with Fire, the reader is invited to consult the book for the *Minchiate Tarot*.

Divinatory meaning: Vigor, strength, might, power. Forcefulness and triumph, for good or ill, is the message of the Ace of Swords. Intellectual or philosophical passion, uncompromising ideals, fierce idealism.

23 — *Two of Swords*

TWO OF SWORDS

23-1, *Ship of Fools Tarot*

An old, blindfolded fool sits unconcerned while a pair of young boys resort to daggers and swords during a game of cards (23-1). This image is a close copy of a *Narrenschiff* illustration that criticizes the lax teaching of children (*Von ler der kind**)(23-2). The scene takes place in a room equipped with a lavabo and hanging hand towel. An

---

*   Of the Rearing of Children: "He who watches the mischief and devilment / Of his children indulgently, sparing the rod, / To him much sorrow will come in the end."

open door shows an angle of a typical medieval street. The pips of the *Tarot de Marseille* are always straightforward, decorative designs: the Two of Swords will show, for example, two crossed swords, perhaps embellished with floral tracery or intertwined ribbons. It seems superfluous therefore to illustrate and describe the *Marseille* numbered cards in detail here. In contrast, the pips of the *Waite-Smith* series, in a true Tarot innovation, contain vivid scenes. The Two of Swords presents a blindfolded woman who sits alone on a stool, her back to the open sea (23-3). She holds two large swords crossed at her breast. Both the *Waite* and the *Ship of Fools* cards suggest immanent danger, quiet and foreboding in the former, raucous and senseless in the second.

Divinatory meaning: Unstable situation, immanent peril. Standoff or uneasy truce. Unbridled childishness, adult neglect. An abdication of guardianship, willful blindness. Lunatics running the asylum. Disaster averted, but more by luck than merit.

23-2, *Narrenschiff*

23-3, *Rider-Waite Tarot*

24 — *Three of Swords*

THREE OF SWORDS

24-1, *Ship of Fools Tarot*

In another image taken in toto from the *Narrenschiff*, the Three of Swords card of the *Ship of Fools Tarot* shows a smiling woman who cuts the hair of a sleeping man: Samson and Delilah (24-1, 2). This illustration comes from a chapter by Brant on the importance of keeping secrets (*Heymlicheit verswigen**). The three swords of the card

---

* Keeping Secrets: "He who cannot keep his silence / And must divulge his plans to another / Will suffer regret, harm, and sorrow."

title are Samson's sheathed sword and the two blades of Delilah's scissors. The *Waite-Smith* card, inspired by a decorated card from the antique *Sola-Busca* series, has a heart pierced through by three swords against a backdrop of rain clouds (24-3). The *Waite-Smith* card is an emblem of woe; the *Ship of Fools* card is humorous and amorous.

Divinatory meaning: Dangerous romance, amorous difficulties, misunderstandings in love. Secrets revealed, surprising reversals, tables turned. Victory of the underdog; alertness defeats complacency. Comeuppance: pride goeth before a bad haircut.

24-2, *Narrenschiff*

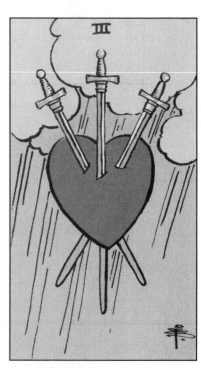

24-3, *Rider-Waite Tarot*

25 — Four of Swords

FOUR OF SWORDS

25-1, *Ship of Fools Tarot*

A crowd of four fools raise swords against each other in a dispute over farm animals (25-1). Once again the image has come entirely from Brant's book, except for the crucial addition of the suit signs (25-2). The *Narrenschiff* image describes the folly of borrowing too much (*Von zuo borg vff nemen**). The *Ship of Fools* card escalates the

---

* Of Excessive Borrowing: "He who borrows too much / On the due date shall see the ravenous wolf / And feel the kick of the donkey as well."

strife from fisticuffs to swordplay. Entirely different is the *Waite-Smith* design, which contains a knightly tomb flanked by one sword on a sarcophagus; three more swords hang on the wall next to a stained glass window (25-3). The *Waite* image is one of funereal sadness; the *Ship of Fools* one of chaotic combat.

Divinatory meaning: Arguments, contention, bickering. Dispute between friends and partners, disagreements over ownership. Neither a borrower nor a lender be, especially in an armed population.

25-2, *Narrenschiff*

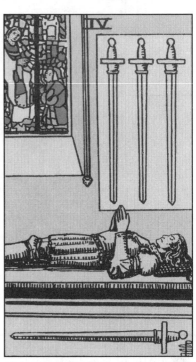

25-3, *Rider-Waite Tarot*

26 — *Five of Swords*

FIVE OF SWORDS

26-1, *Ship of Fools Tarot*

In a setting of a deserted village street, a sly-looking fool holds three swords (26-1). Two more lie on the ground before him. No single *Narrenschiff* design contributed to the card, instead the *Waite-Smith* image inspired our card. In Smith's design a smiling, windblown young man holds three swords in his two hands (26-2). Nearby two additional swords lie unclaimed at his feet. Two distant human figures, one with his head in his hands, lend a sense of melancholy to the scene. Jagged clouds overhead add another element of unease.

Divinatory Meaning: A quiet victory. Winning by default. Triumph as the result of the retreat or disappearance of the opponent. Victory goes, sometimes, to the one who merely shows up.

26-2, *Rider-Waite Tarot*

SIX OF SWORDS

27-1, *Ship of Fools Tarot*

𝔄 worried fool struggles with the rigging of his small boat in the Six of Swords (27-1). His vessel is breaking apart, and the shore is at some distance, so the fool should indeed be concerned. The image follows closely one from Brant that admonishes those who decry misfortune, or who foolishly seek out mischance (*Verachtung vngfelles**)

---

* Contempt of Misfortune: "A fool is the man who does not understand / That mishaps lead him by the hand, / That he should wisely give himself over; / Misfortune will not be disdained."

(27-2). Only the six swords embedded in the planks of the boat have been added for our card. The *Waite-Smith* card also shows a boat—it too is pierced with standing swords (27-3). A young boatman poles the boat forward while a heavily shrouded figure, flanked by a child, sits huddled below. The *Waite* card is sad and quiet; the *Ship of Fools* version is wild and unsettled.

Divinatory meaning: A passage or journey—fraught with difficulties perhaps, but ultimately successful. Struggling to keep things together, trying to keep one's vessel afloat. Rough seas, high winds. Even a leaky ship can get to shore.

27-2, *Narrenschiff*

27-3, *Rider-Waite Tarot*

28 — Seven of Swords

28-1, *Ship of Fools Tarot*

𝕬 fool carries five swords on his shoulders (28-1). He springs forward and looks back in a way that suggests flight. The fool and his doorway have been adapted from a *Narrenschiff* illustration of strife and discord (*Von zwytracht machen*) (28-2). The real source of the image is of course the corresponding *Waite-Smith* card, where a prancing man escapes with five swords as two other swords remain planted in the ground (28-3). He smiles over his shoulder at an encampment of tents.

Divinatory meaning: Stealth and furtiveness. An attempted caper, theft, or scheme. Success by trickery.

28-2, *Narrenschiff*

28-3, *Rider-Waite Tarot*

29 — *Eight of Swords*

29-1, *Ship of Fools Tarot*

Overloaded boats, thronged with fools, sail together on the card of the Eight of Swords (29-1). The original *Narrenschiff* image, without an accompanying verse, titled *Eyn gessellen schiff*, has been reframed, and six fools have been given swords to augment the enormous pair of scissors held by another (29-2). The *Waite-Smith* card, in contrast, portrays a bound and blindfolded woman who stands surrounded by swords ominously stuck in the ground (29-3).

Divinatory meaning: Directionless journey, wayward voyage, aimless motion. A mission or crusade. Collective endeavor, group effort. Festivity, merrymaking. Messing about in boats.

29-2, *Narrenschiff*   29-3, *Rider-Waite Tarot*

30 — Nine of Swords

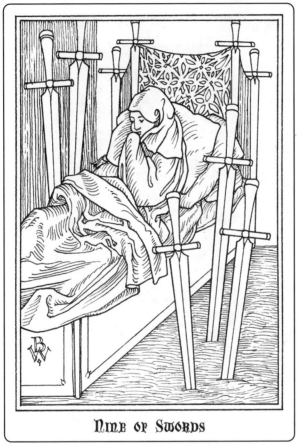

NINE OF SWORDS

30-1, *Ship of Fools Tarot*

A shrouded figure sits up in bed and covers part of her face in the Nine of Swords card (30-1). A cluster of swords, jammed into the floor, hem her in. Her bed comes from a *Narrenschiff* print that warns about judging others, but the real inspiration for our card is again the *Waite-Smith* Nine of Swords, in which a figure sits up in bed and covers her (or his) face in apparent dismay or fear. A row of nine swords, parallel and horizontal, hang above on a black wall (30-2).

Divinatory meaning: Worries, fears. Preoccupations, distress. Insomnia or nightmares. Things going bump in the night.

30-2, *Rider-Waite Tarot*

31 — Ten of Swords

TEN OF SWORDS

31-1, *Ship of Fools Tarot*

A fool prepares to strike a supine figure in the design for the Ten of Swords (31-1). His frightened opponent has a sword, as do eight intent onlookers. The image, sans swords, illustrates the stupid cruelty of false friends in Brant's book (*Von worer fruntschaft**) (31-2). The

---

* Of True Friendship: "He who does violence and injustice / To one who has done him no wrong / Earns the ill will of all others."

Waite-Smith Ten of Swords shows an unfortunate victim who lies on the ground, impaled by ten standing swords (31-3).

Divinatory meaning: Setback, reversal, difficulty. Bullying, betrayal. False friends, unhelpful onlookers. With friends like these. . . .

31-2, *Narrenschiff*

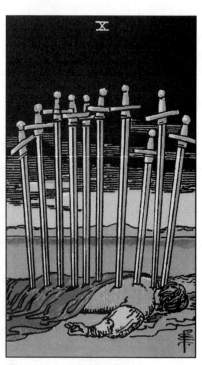

31-3, *Rider-Waite Tarot*

32 — Page of Swords

32-1, *Ship of Fools Tarot*

The Page of Swords holds his sword and sticks out his tongue on his *Ship of Fools* card (32-1). His sword was originally a staff in the *Narrenschiff* illustration, where the figure illustrates "Of idle chatter" (*Von vil schwetzen**) (32-2). The Page of the *Tarot de Marseille* is a well-dressed youth with both a sword and a slender staff (32-3). Pixie

---

* Of Idle Chatter: "He who keeps guard over tongue and mouth / Steels his soul against fear and despair: / The woodpecker's cry betrays his young."

32-2, *Narrenschiff*

32-3, *Tarot de Marseille*

32-4, *Rider-Waite Tarot*

Smith's Page is a bareheaded young man who holds up his sword with both hands (32-4). His pose suggests optimism and energy, his hair blows in the wind. Great white clouds fill the background.

Divinatory meaning: A dynamic and energetic person, prepared to embark on any endeavor. A sharp-tongued individual, a fork-tongued persuader, a charming chatterer.

33 — Knight of Swords

33-1, *Ship of Fools Tarot*

A fool rides a stern donkey and holds up his sword on the *Ship of Fools* Knight of Swords (33-1). The *Marseille* version wears armor and rides a rearing horse (33-2). The *Waite-Smith* knight charges full force, his sword ready to strike, his face intent on his adversaries (33-3). The *Ship of Fools* knight differs from the others in obvious ways: he wears a fool's attire, not armor; he rides a donkey, not a horse. His smiling face doesn't threaten.

Divinatory meaning: A fearless and daring person. A headstrong, impetuous character, ready to charge off to save the world. A Don Quixote, tilting at windmills.

33-2, *Tarot de Marseille*

33-3 *Rider-Waite Tarot*

34 — Queen of Swords

QUEEN OF SWORDS

34-1, *Ship of Fools Tarot*

A tall, slender Queen of Swords drags a fool's cap along the floor of a well-furnished domestic interior (34-1). Our card follows closely an illustration in Brant criticizing bad manners (*Von bosen sytten**), where, however, the figure is a beardless youth (34-2). The queen of the *Tarot de Marseille* sits in an enveloping throne (34-3). The *Waite-*

---

* Of Poor Manners: "He who is of coarse manner and custom / To the point that he becomes a fool, / He drags the fool's cap along the floor."

34-2, *Narrenschiff*

REGINA DI SPADE

34-3, *Tarot de Marseille*

QUEEN of SWORDS.

34-4, *Rider-Waite Tarot*

Smith queen, serious and serene, is shown seated in profile (34-4). She gestures with her left arm and rests the hilt of her upright sword on the arm of her carved throne. Butterfly motifs adorn her iron crown and stone chair. The scene is set outdoors against an open sky and low-lying cumulus clouds. Tarot queens and kings usually sit in thrones; *Ship of Fools* royalty usually stand.

Divinatory meaning: A perceptive and clear-sighted person, penetrating, incisive, persuasive. Unconcerned about conventional opinion, an independent thinker. Passionate and deep. A firebrand, given to Joan of Arc crusades or Antigone causes.

35 — King of Swords

KING OF SWORDS

35-1, *Ship of Fools Tarot*

The King of Swords, a mature, beardless man, stands with his sword sheathed at his belt (35-1). A fool holds him by the shoulder, as if tempting him to folly. The original *Narrenschiff* image accompanies a chapter about those who would erroneously work or play on the Sabbath (*Von verfuerung am fyrtag**) (35-2). The *Marseille*

---

* Of Being Misguided on Holidays: "On holy days men should go to church / And leave their labors at home / And yet many search for business."

35-2, *Narrenschiff*

35-3, *Tarot de Marseille*

35-4, *Rider-Waite Tarot*

King, clean-shaven and youthful, is shown as expected: seated, wearing armor, and sporting a very large, broad-brimmed, crowned hat (35-3). The mature and beardless king of the *Waite-Smith* card is also seated, but does not wear armor (35-4). His throne is invisible except for a high, narrow tapestry behind him. As for the other members of his court, a grand sky is his backdrop.

Divinatory meaning: A person of expansive and explosive temperament, a fighter and leader. The active, as opposed to the contemplative, approach to life. An over-achiever, a never-rester.

36 — Ace of Staves

36-1, *Ship of Fools Tarot*

A fool playfully holds up a large pole or staff on the Ace of Staves card (36-1). A giant fool's cap crowns the staff. The *Tarot de Marseille* and the *Waite-Smith* cards closely resemble each other; Pamela Colman Smith clearly based her aces on the ancient model of a disembodied hand, emerging from clouds, which holds the suit sign (36-2, 3). Staves in the *Ship of Fools Tarot* are usually surmounted by comic fools' heads, while the *Marseille* clubs can be rough cudgels or lathe-turned scepters. The *Waite-Smith* wands, different again, are long slender poles that, ending in leafy twigs, suggest lengths of freshly cut saplings.

Divinatory meaning: Creativity, success, experiment, reform, appreciation of beauty. Power, energy, innovation. A big bang, a big stick, whether one speaks softly or not.

36-2, *Tarot de Marseille*

36-3, *Rider-Waite Tarot*

37 — *Two of Staves*

TWO OF STAVES

37-1, *Ship of Fools Tarot*

The Two of Staves shows a pair of fools who wield staves in an attempt to force a pig into a square basket (37-1). The original image, an illustration for the chapter on good counselors (*Von guten reten**), has a large pot instead of the basket, illustrating the proverb of driving the sow to the rendering vat before it is dead, or putting the

---

* Of Good Counsel: "He who eagerly follows the counsel of the wise, / But then follows it wherever the wind may lead, / He tries to put the sow in the kettle before she's dead."

cart before the horse (37-2). The *Waite-Smith* image instead is of a man in his prime who faces out on a distant coastline from a high castle wall (37-3). He studies a world globe, which he holds close; he grasps a staff in his left hand. A second staff stands alongside.

Divinatory meaning: Potential riches and success, but the danger of counting one's chickens before they're hatched. Excitement, enthusiasm, feverish activity. Cooperation, teamwork, constructive endeavor. Two fools are better than one.

37-2, *Narrenschiff*

37-3, *Rider-Waite Tarot*

38 — Three of Staves

THREE OF STAVES

38-1, *Ship of Fools Tarot*

A barefoot fool, standing in an empty village street, plays a bagpipe on the card of the Three of Staves (38-1). Two musical instruments, a lute and a harp, lie at his feet. The original image from Brant's book, illustrating "On impatience of retribution" (*Von Ungedult der Straff**), has been altered by turning the three pipes of the fool's instrument into fools' staves (38-2). Smith's design includes a

---

* On Impatience of Retribution: "If you rejoice in vulgar pipes, / And harps and lutes disdain, / You ride in carts with fools."

solitary male figure, seen from behind, who looks out at the sea from a high wild place (38-3). Two staves stand alone; he holds up a third.

Divinatory meaning: Prosperity, ease, relaxation. Music, leisure, and repose. The consolations of music; bagpipes soothe the savage beast.

38-2, *Narrenschiff*

38-3, *Rider-Waite Tarot*

39 — Four of Staves

FOUR OF STAVES

39-1, *Ship of Fools Tarot*

𝕬 swirling banner flutters above a fool and a young dandy (39-1). Each man holds two staves. The original *Narrenschiff* image lacks the four's staves and includes instead a small round mirror that the fool offers to the fashionably dressed young man, in a critique of novelty (*Von nuwen funden**) (39-2). The Four of Wands from the *Waite-*

---

* Of Novelties: "He who spreads innovation through the land / Only creates shame and nuisance / And holds the fool by the hand."

Smith pack is an outdoor scene with four straight-standing poles (39-3). A large garland hangs between them, creating an open canopy or gateway. Far beyond small human figures wave bunches of flowers, suggesting celebration. Castle walls rise in the distance.

Divinatory meaning: Celebration, festivity. Social ceremony, public rite, community holiday. Flag-waving, baton-twirling, banner-swirling. Innovations, fads, fashion. Clothes make the fool.

39-2, *Narrenschiff*

39-3, *Rider-Waite Tarot*

40 — *Five of Staves*

FIVE OF STAVES

40-1, *Ship of Fools Tarot*

Four fools, brandishing staves, descend threateningly on two calm dignitaries, one of whom holds another staff. (40-1). The original illustration appears twice in the *Narrenschiff*, to admonish "scorners" (*Von spott vogelen**) and "prevention of the good" (*Hyndernys des gutten*) (40-2). The corresponding card in *Waite-Smith* includes five

---

* Of Stone Throwers: "It is wise to avoid the fool / Who always pelts with rocks / Ignoring both ill and wisdom."

young men brandishing five large wands, whether in sport or combat is unclear (40-3).

Divinatory meaning: Quarrels and argument. Calm reason opposed to emotional intensity. Mob mentality, hooliganism, team sports.

40-2, *Narrenschiff*

40-3, *Rider-Waite Tarot*

41 — Six of Staves

SIX OF STAVES

41-1, *Ship of Fools Tarot*

fool sits sprawled on a donkey and waves a staff while a woman on her knees pulls on the animal's tail (41-1). A small crowd waves five staves in the background; in the foreground a little dog yaps at the fool. Once again the *Narrenschiff* illustration appears twice in Brant's book: to describe "ready anger" (*Von luchtlich zyrnen**), and

---

* Of Ready Anger: "He who always spurs the ass / Will end up head over heels above the donkey's ears / Swift anger well befits the fool."

"bad women" (*Von bosen wibern***) (41-2). In this original image the fool waves a small whip, not a fool's staff. A staff-waving crowd has been added to the scene for our tarot card. Rather than an undignified fool, the analogous *Waite-Smith* figure is a proud young man, crowned with laurel, who rides his horse in apparent triumph (41-3). He holds a wand adorned with a second wreath; five more wands wave above the heads of onlookers behind the rider.

Divinatory meaning: An uneasy success, a contested victory. Advancement hindered by controversy and polemics. A celebration gone awry; rain on the victory parade.

** Of Bad Women: "Many a man would ride night and day / To escape the clutches of this woman / But the ass will seldom grant him peace."

41-2, *Narrenschiff*   41-3, *Rider-Waite Tarot*

42 — Seven of Staves

42-1, *Ship of Fools Tarot*

One fool struggles with his cap, another places a bell and collar on a cat, while around them swirls a chaos of staves and romping dogs (42-1). A broad arched opening reveals a glimpse of medieval houses on the left. At the right rear a niche holds a sink. Brant's woodcut for "the libel of the good" (*Hynderred des guten**) provides the design;

---

* Libel of the Good: "Many men chide all others / And hang bells on the cat, / And yet won't hear a word themselves."

only the many staves were added to create the tarot card (42-2). The *Waite-Smith* card presents a single figure in the act of fending off a mass of threatening wands (42-3).

Divinatory meaning: Strife and confusion. Boisterous play, rambunctious frolic. Clamor, tumult, turbulence. Children, pets, and other infernal distractions.

42-2, *Narrenschiff*

42-3, *Rider-Waite Tarot*

43 — Eight of Staves

43-1, *Ship of Fools Tarot*

An interior encloses a scene of domestic strife: a calm woman faces a staff-waving fool (43-1). She holds two staves of her own; a child standing next to her holds another staff and a small jug. Eight staves have been crowded into the scene for the *Ship of Fools Tarot*. In the original image the fool threatens his family with a broken crock and holds out a backgammon board (43-2). Brant ridicules here the bad example that parents give their children (*Bos exemple der eltern**). Eight parallel wands slant across an open sky on the *Waite-Smith* card (43-3). Far away and below lies a hilly landscape.

Divinatory meaning: Disruptions in domestic life, family arguments. Disagreements between partners, between the sexes, or between the generations. Working out differences with frank discussion, airing one's problems in order to resolve them. Screaming, shouting, and breaking things as a negotiating strategy.

---

* Bad Examples Set by Parents: "Children mimic the parents / And copy their shameless ways; / If parents break jars, so too do the children."

43-2, *Narrenschiff*

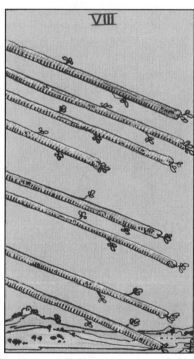

43-3, *Rider-Waite Tarot*

44 — *Nine of Staves*

NINE OF STAVES

44-1, *Ship of Fools Tarot*

A fool charges forward with a staff in his hands (44-1). Behind him stands an uneven screen of high staves planted in an open field. The figure is taken from a *Narrenschiff* illustration of a "blaspheming" fool (*Von gottes lestern*) (44-2). Calmer is the sturdy peasant or foot soldier, in Pixie Smith's design, who rests with his tall wand in front of an imposing fence of eight more staves (44-3).

Divinatory meaning: Vigilance, readiness, alertness. Defensive posture, protective stance. Strength awaiting its test. Vigilance is the price of paranoia.

44-2, *Narrenschiff*

44-3, *Rider-Waite Tarot*

45-1, *Ship of Fools Tarot*

A grimacing fool struggles under the weight of a bundle of ten staves in the *Ship of Fools* card of that title (45-1). In Brant's book he labors under a heavy sack, while two more overwhelm his donkey (45-2). This fool suffers from having too much of a good thing, as Brant chastises those who accept too many benefices (*Von vile der pfrunden**). Also burdened with a bundle of heavy sticks is the man in the *Waite-Smith* Ten of Wands (45-3).

Divinatory meaning: Burdens and worries, but not insuperable ones. Too much of a good thing. Unseemly excess. Biting off more than one can chew with one's mouth closed.

---

* Of Excessive Indulgences: "He who believes he needs indulgences on the earth / Will cause his ass to trip more often than proceed: / Too much baggage will be the death of the mule."

45-2, *Narrenschiff*

45-3, *Rider-Waite Tarot*

46 — *The Page of Staves*

PAGE OF STAVES

46-1, *Ship of Fools Tarot*

Our Page of Staves blows a hunting horn and carries a long staff (46-1). He stands in a wild place where rabbits, chased by a small dog, dash about. A glance at the *Narrenschiff* print reveals that only the staff, originally a spear, has been changed (46-2). Once again a single image has been used more than once in Brant's book, in this case to condemn "serving two masters" (*Von dienst zweyer herren**),

---

* Of Serving Two Masters: "He who tries to hunt two hares at once / While in the service of two masters / Has truly bitten off more than he can chew."

46-2, *Narrenschiff*

46-3, *Tarot de Marseille*

46-4 *Rider-Waite Tarot*

and "useless hunting" (*Von vnnutzen jagen***). The *Tarot de Marseille* Page holds his large staff, upright and resting on the ground, with both hands (46-3). He wears the hat, belted tunic, and slashed oversleeves familiar from other *Marseille* cards. Typical of the *Waite-Smith* images is the slender, well-dressed, poised young man who, like the *Marseille* page, holds his wand upright with both hands and with the end of the staff resting on the earth (46-4).

Divinatory meaning: A smart and poised, helpful and compassionate person. A messenger, a bearer of good news; a musician; a hunter.

** Of Useless Hunting: "Many a man spends great sums on the hunt / That nonetheless brings him little of use, / No matter how loud he shout out the hunter's call"

47 — Knight of Staves

47-1, *Ship of Fools Tarot*

A happy jester, holding his fool's staff, rides his donkey in a rolling landscape (47-1). The image brings together elements from different *Narrenschiff* illustrations. The calm *Marseille* knight holds up his customary cudgel (47-2). His horse is heavily draped. The alert and earnest *Waite-Smith* Knight of Wands sits astride a rearing horse (47-3). He too holds his suit sign. His helmet is plumed, his cloak decorated with black salamanders.

Divinatory meaning: A feisty, stern person. Impetuous but courteous, headstrong and impassioned. A traveler, especially one who departs or withdraws.

47-2, *Tarot de Marseille*

47-3, *Rider-Waite Tarot*

48 — Queen of Staves

ꝊUᴇᴇꝊ Oꝑ SᴛꝸꝊᴇꜱ

48-1, *Ship of Fools Tarot*

The Queen of Staves wears a crown and holds a slender staff, the only details of the card changed from the *Narrenschiff* original (48-1, 2). She also holds curious leashes that lead out to bind a bird, a sheep, and a bull. A fool pulls on the tails of the latter two animals. Brant's female figure therefore is a personification of slavery to sensual appetite (*Von wollust**). The *Marseille* queen is seated, as is customary,

---

* Of Decadent Lust: "Lust and hedonism often fell the simple / Who are thus held in flight, / Many have in this wise chosen their end."

48-2, *Narrenschiff*

48-3, *Tarot de Marseille*

48-4, *Rider-Waite Tarot*

and holds a large, top-heavy scepter (48-3). Pamela Colman Smith's queen is a young woman who holds her slender rustic wand in one hand and a sunflower in the other (48-4). She sits, gazing off to the side, on a stone throne flanked by carved lions. A tapestry decorated with small rampant lions is at her back. A mountainous desert is her distant backdrop. At front and center a black cat sits alert, looking out at us.

Divinatory meaning: A creative and intelligent person, extroverted and active. A charismatic presence that attracts one and all. A lover of creatures, animal and human.

49 — King of Staves

KING OF STAVES

49-1, *Ship of Fools Tarot*

The King of Staves stands alongside a fool who is blowing in his ear: that is, whispering lies (49-1). The king's suit sign and his crown have been added to the original image, "on blowing into ears" (*Von oren blosen**) (49-2). The seated *Tarot de Marseille* king, young and beardless, holds a double-ended scepter (49-3). The young *Waite-*

---

* On Blowing into Ears: "A sign of gullibility it is / To believe anything one is told; / A prattler may easily deceive many."

49-2, *Narrenschiff*

49-3 *Tarot de Marseille*

49-4, *Rider-Waite Tarot*

Smith King of Wands is also clean-shaven (49-4). He sits in profile on a throne backed with designs of lions and salamanders. A live salamander can be seen at the king's feet.

Divinatory meaning: A brilliant, innovative, creative person. An inventor or artist, one who brings the new to life. One receptive to new ideas, to advice, to getting an earful.

50 — Ace of Cups

ACE OF CUPS

50-1, *The Ship of Fools Tarot*

A fool waves in jubilation—or alarm—from within a giant drinking cup on the Ace of Cups (50-1). He holds up another cup and gazes upward at a floating crown. Part of the image is borrowed from a *Narrenschiff* illustration in which a fool has trapped himself in a well, the print for "on courting misfortune" (*Von mutwilligem vngfell*) (50-2). The *Tarot de Marseille* Ace of Cups is an elaborate covered chalice that fills its frame (50-3). The *Waite-Smith* version centers on

50-2, *Narrenschiff*

50-3, *Tarot de Marseille*

50-4, *Rider-Waite Tarot*

a tall chalice that rests in the upturned palm of a celestial hand (50-4). The dove of the Holy Spirit, holding the Eucharist in its beak, points itself toward the cup from above. The bowl of the cup is inscribed with the letter "W." Four slender streams of water jump from the chalice and fall into an endless sea below, where lily pads float.

The Ace of Cups announces a superabundance of the gifts, and the dangers, associated with water and wine: rejoicing, celebration, conviviality, cleansing, but also drunkenness and loss of control. The suit of Cups has long been connected with the emotions. The Ace therefore suggests a heart bursting with love, or conversely one overwhelmed, drowning in emotion.

Divinatory meaning: Overflowing emotion, abundant love. My heart runneth over: plentiful joy. Happiness and fulfillment. Contentment and gratification in the affections. Obsession with emotions, preoccupation with issues of the heart.

51 — Two of Cups

51-1, *Ship of Fools Tarot*

A dandy and a young woman toast each other on the Two of Cups
(51-1). The image differs from its source in the *Narrenschiff* in
that the two figures have been given cups and the young man's falcon
has been removed (51-2). Unchanged are the three dogs in the foreground, for the original image mocks those who bring animals to
church (*Gebracht in der kirchen**). The corresponding card of the

---

* Unholy Din in Church: "He who takes birds and dogs to church / Disturbing
others who would fain pray, / He flatters and cajoles the cuckoo."

Waite-Smith series shows a young couple, wreathed like newlyweds, who raise a toast to each other below a floating emblem of a lion-headed caduceus (51-3).

Divinatory meaning: First love, love at first sight, a new romance. Mutual happiness, affectionate gratitude. Amorous attraction, exciting beginnings. Unrealistic expectations, idealistic affections. There is no fool like a fool in love.

51-2, *Narrenschiff*

51-3, *Rider-Waite Tarot*

52 — Three of Cups

THREE OF CUPS

52-1, *Ship of Fools Tarot*

Three young women, hooded with fools' caps, hold their cups before a closed door (52-1). The original *Narrenschiff* image has them holding oil lamps, and includes a flaming demon's head devouring a sinner in the middle ground (52-2). Refraining from good works (*Ablossung gutter werck**) is the subject of the original woodblock. On the *Waite-Smith* card three maidens, looking like the Three

---

* Abstaining from Good Works: "He who lights his lantern well / And lets its oil burn bright / He shall enjoy eternal delight."

Graces of classical antiquity, dance and toast each other in a bed of flowers (52-3).

Divinatory meaning: Gracefulness, abundance, rejoicing, harmony, balance. Friendship and companionship. A balanced trio, a balanced triad. Social graces, a convivial dance of family, friends, or lovers. Dancing until dizzy, toasting until toasted.

52-2, *Narrenschiff*

52-3, *Rider-Waite Tarot*

53 — Four of Cups

FOUR OF CUPS

53-1, *Ship of Fools Tarot*

𝕬 fool has nodded off before his small fire on the Four of Cups (53-1). Three cups stand on the ground; a fourth is about to be emptied onto the fool's head by a celestial hand. The scene has been adapted from a *Narrenschiff* image that satirizes sloth (*Von tragheit vnd fulheit**) as an alert hunter or pilgrim strides past the sleeping fool

---

* Of Indolence and Sloth: "Laziness can be found among all the classes / Especially among maids and servants; / No matter how much their remuneration / They will not so much as lift a finger."

(53-2). Pamela Colman Smith's image shows a young man who doesn't sleep, but seems to be refusing the chalice offered him by a cloud-enshrouded hand (53-3). The *Waite-Smith* meaning seems to be that an opportunity or responsibility is being resisted; the *Ship of Fools* card shows that laziness or inattention may be punished with an abrupt awakening.

Divinatory meaning: Sloth, lassitude, laziness. Procrastination. Hesitation, reflection. Rest, retreat, restoring one's forces. A rude awakening, a needed jolt, an end to noodling.

53-2, *Narrenschiff*

53-3, *Rider-Waite Tarot*

54 — Five of Cups

FIVE OF CUPS

54-1, *Ship of Fools Tarot*

𝔄 fool has come upon a scene of feeding farm animals on the Five of Cups (54-1). The image differs from the *Narrenschiff* original only in that a long trough has been turned into four tubs, which, with the cup hanging from the fool's neck, provide the five cups needed for the card (54-2). Insolence toward God is the subject of the original image (*Von versmessenheit gotz**). The Five of Cups in the *Waite-*

---

* Of Impudence before God: "He who wails that God has no mercy / And shows no justice, / He has the reason of geese and sows."

Smith pack shows a lone figure, head bowed, darkly shrouded, seen from behind in a desolate landscape (54-3). At his or her feet three cups have been overturned, their contents spilled, while on his right two more cups stand upright.

Divinatory meaning: An undignified feeding frenzy. Bounty, but of a rustic or disordered kind. Country life, rural work, pastoral pastime. Some of the resources on hand have been devoured, but some remains in reserve.

54-2, *Narrenschiff*

54-3, *Rider-Waite Tarot*

55 — Six of Cups

55-1, *Ship of Fools Tarot*

A child riding a hobbyhorse and a standing fool toast each other on the Six of Cups (55-1). Four additional cups are lined up in the foreground. A third figure accompanies them in the original image, a fool drawing his sword; he has been removed, and the cups added, for the *Ship of Fools* card. "Not taking a joke" (*Schympf nit verston**) is the

---

* Not Taking a Joke: "He who consorts with child and fool / Must also wink at their jests, / Otherwise he'll join the fools."

original subject (55-2). A small boy hands an even smaller girl a large cup brimming with flowers in the *Waite-Smith* image (55-3). Four more bouquets in four chalices line the bottom of the image, while a sixth chalice sits on a plinth by a stone staircase beside the children. A grand medieval manor rises behind.

Divinatory meaning: Happy childhood, childlike play and pleasure. Memory, nostalgia. Nurturing and mentoring. Childish games, inappropriate in an adult, but fun.

55-2, *Narrenschiff*

55-3, *Rider-Waite Tarot*

56 — *Seven of Cups*

SEVEN OF CUPS

56-1, *Ship of Fools Tarot*

An alchemist-fool tends a boiling pan in the Seven of Cups (56-1). A rather pompous worthy holds a cup and stands at the alchemist's shoulder; an undignified fool holds another cup while sprawling above a barrel (56-2). Five more cups and a chemist's retort lie on the floor below the fireplace. The image differs from the *Narrenschiff* version, on falsity and deception (more strongly worded in the original!)

(*Von falsch vnd beschiss***), primarily in the addition of the extra cups (56-2). In the *Waite-Smith* card a shadowy image gestures in awe at a floating vision of seven chalices, each of which brims with a different prize, or danger: a pretty face; a small shrouded figure; a serpent; a miniature castle; glittering riches; a laurel wreath; and a dragon (56-3).

Divinatory meaning: Magical operations, arcane experiments, alchemical investigations. Fantasy and imagination. Pursuing exalted dreams, building sky castles, chasing wild geese.

---

* Of Falsity and Bullshit: "With alchemy, as well as with / The science of the vines, / One senses how much nonsense / And false knowledge there is on the earth."

56-2, *Narrenschiff*

56-3, *Rider-Waite Tarot*

57 — *Eight of Cups*

EIGHT OF CUPS

57-1, *Ship of Fools Tarot*

A busy fool stirs a large cook pot or cauldron on the Eight of Cups (57-1). He holds a cup in one hand and rests a large staff in the crook of his arm. All around him are arranged seven more vessels and other kitchen objects. A long-nosed cat joins him at the great fireplace. The image has been taken in its entirety, except for the addition of the extra cups, from an illustration in the *Narrenschiff* that satirizes self-complacency (*Von im selbs wolgefafallen**), where the fool holds a looking glass instead of a cup (57-2). The image drawn by Pamela Colman Smith includes a row of cups in the foreground, three stacked on five, and a human figure who is walking, his back turned, toward a distant mountainous landscape. He uses a walking stick. The human face of the Moon looks down on the scene from an otherwise empty sky (57-3).

Divinatory meaning: Domestic activity, busy homemaking. Cooking and cuisine. Concocting new solutions, cooking up a new approach. If ill favored, the card may mean turning one's backs on projects and goals.

---

* Of Self-Satisfaction: "In the fool's brew I must steep: / Since I cherish my own reflection, / I am brother to the ass."

57-2, Narrenschiff

57-3, Rider-Waite Tarot

58 — *Nine of Cups*

ℕ𝕚𝕟𝕖 𝕠𝕗 ℂ𝕦𝕡𝕤

58-1, *Ship of Fools Tarot*

𝒜 crowd of fools carouses around a tavern table on the card of the Nine of Cups (58-1). The image comes directly, except for the additional cups, from a *Narrenschiff* illustration that criticizes spend-thrift ways and luxurious living (*Von fullen vnd prassen**) (58-2). In the *Waite-Smith* image a stout, well-dressed burgher folds his hands

---

* Of Gluttony and Profligacy: "He rightly falls into certain future poverty, / Who always craves pretension and excess, / And keeps company with spendthrifts."

in self-satisfaction and sits before a draped counter covered with a line of nine large goblets (58-3).

Divinatory meaning: Festive company, convivial gathering. Prosperity, generosity. Rejoicing and feasting—sometimes, vulgar carousing and superficial festivity.

58-2, *Narrenschiff*

58-3, *Rider-Waite Tarot*

TEN OF CUPS

59-1, *Ship of Fools Tarot*

The Ten of Cups shows a busy street scene (59-1). In the foreground a fool intently plays his lute. Three other fools and a small
child assist him in his serenade. His intended audience, an undressed
lady at a window, shows her displeasure by emptying kitchen slops, or
worse, on the crowd below. The child, who is holding out a cup, seems
in particular danger of being drenched. Once again the image comes
in its entirety from the *Narrenschiff*, "Of nightly serenades" (*Von*

nachtes hofyeren*), except for the addition of many cups (59-2). In the *Waite-Smith* image a "rainbow" of chalices crown a happy couple and a pair of dancing children (59-3).

Divinatory meaning: Reveling and exultation, perhaps to excess. Practical jokes, amusing surprises. Music and song, nocturnal wanderings, evening festivities. Public holidays, general rejoicing.

---

* Of Nightly Serenades: "He who covets minstrel ways / And serenades at night before women's doors / Also invites the frost to sting."

59-2, *Narrenschiff*

59-3, *Rider-Waite Tarot*

60 — *Page of Cups*

60-1, *Ship of Fools Tarot*

The Page of Cups, a fool holding a drinking cup, struggles to walk in the marshy margins of a country road, water grasses and cattails around his knees (60-1). The fool points to a roadside shrine that holds a crucifix. Another hand that emerges from the shrine points to the true path, the sensible way: the route that the fool has not taken. Exactly the same is the original *Narrenschiff* image, for "Of paths

60-2, *Narrenschiff*

60-3, *Tarot de Marseille*

60-4, *Rider-Waite Tarot*

blazed alone" (*Von stroffen un selb tun**), except that the fool's staff has been replaced with a cup (60-2). The Page of Cups from the *Tarot de Marseille* is an elaborately dressed young man who carries a large covered goblet (60-3). The *Waite-Smith* youth is similar, though more naturalistically drawn (60-4). He wears a fifteenth-century costume and smiles at a small fish that peeks out of his chalice. Water ripples behind him.

The *Ship of Fools* page has forsaken the beaten path, he has strayed from the proper road. He incurs thereby all the dangers of becoming lost, of bogging down in mud, or even quicksand. On the way, though, he's sure to have experiences that a sanctioned route would never provide him. He'll find unexpected, extraordinary, enlightening things— at least the lessons learned from failure, or even the feel of creepy-crawlies between his toes.

Divinatory meaning: A wanderer, impulsive quester, wayward pilgrim. An emotional and poetic person, a seeker on life's journey. Side trips and detours, the unexpected moments of travel, the pleasures and perils of a poor sense of direction. Rediscovering one's intended path.

---

* Of Paths Blazed Alone: "He who sees a clear path / And yet lingers in the puddles and moss / Is bare of sense and wisdom."

61 — Knight of Cups

KNIGHT OF CUPS

61-1, *Ship of Fools Tarot*

The Knight of Cups is a grim-faced fool who leans on a slender reed with one hand and holds up his emblem with the other (61-1). His mount is an enormous lobster. A bird swoops down, perilously close to colliding with the fool. Once again a *Narrenschiff* print has been followed closely, this time that for "God's Providence" (*Furwissenheyt gottes**) (61-2). The *Marseille* Knight is a young, bareheaded

---

* God's Providence: "He who, without service, seeks reward / And wishes to stand on a weak limb, / His plans will scuttle backward like the crab's."

61-2, *Narrenschiff*

61-3, *Tarot de Marseille*

61-4, *Rider-Waite Tarot*

rider who holds his large cup in his right hand and the reins in his left (61-3). The proud young man of the *Waite-Smith* deck is dressed in armor (61-4). He holds up his expected tribute; both he and his mount are shown in dignified profile.

Divinatory meaning: A stormy character, a tempestuous person, irascible but true-hearted. Travel, especially across water. A dreamer, whose thoughts go inward.

62 — Queen of Cups

QUEEN OF CUPS

62-1, *Ship of Fools Tarot*

The Queen of Cups smiles and holds up her cup, as if offering it to the fool seated with her at a table (62-1). He covers his face with his left hand. A second cup and several small objects lie before them. Under the table a cat chases three mice, another mouse already in its mouth. In the original *Narrenschiff* image the woman is a straying wife whose husband, a fool, turns a blind eye (*Von eebruch**) (62-2). For the

---

* Of Adultery: "He who peeks through his fingers / And lets his wife consort with other men, / There the cat eyes the mice with glee."

62-2, *Narrenschiff*

62-3, *Tarot de Marseille*

62-4, *Rider-Waite Tarot*

Ship of Fools Tarot she has been given a crown to wear and she has lost the straw with which to tease the fool. The *Marseille* Queen of Cups sits on a throne and holds her cup and a scepter (62-3). The young queen of the *Waite-Smith* card is a brooding beauty who gazes intently at a heavy, elaborate, almost grotesque, covered cup (62-4). Her hair is braided under a large square crown, her throne is a massive stone-carved chair decorated with putti and surmounted by a scallop shell arch. Amphitrite, mistress of mermaids, is the classical goddess of the sea, and thus can be associated with the Queen of Cups, ruler of the watery element.

Divinatory meaning: A lively, engaging, sensual person; one of fluid manner, sparkling surface, profound depths. Emotional depth and psychological insight. Prone to the deepest emotions.

63 — *King of Cups*

KING OF CUPS

63-1, *Ship of Fools Tarot*

The King of Cups is a distinguished, bearded old man who wears a long fur-trimmed robe (63-1). He holds his emblem cup while a young fool seems tentatively to be reaching for it. Three small details transform the image from the *Narrenschiff* original for "Giving and Regretting" (*Schenken vnd beruwen**): the fool has lost a bag of

---

* Giving and Regretting: "He is truly a fool who all day laments / That which he cannot change, / Or mourns a good deed he has done, / To one who cannot understand it."

63-2, *Narrenschiff*

63-3, *Tarot de Marseille*

63-4, *Rider-Waite Tarot*

money, and the old man has gained the cup and crown (63-2). The *Marseille* and *Waite-Smith* kings are both seated, and both hold the expected emblems (63-3, 4). The former's most distinctive feature is his broad-brimmed, crowned hat. He is also bearded. The clean-shaven *Waite-Smith* king rests both arms on the armrests of a throne carved in smooth curves. An Egyptian papyrus motif adorns both his chair and scepter. Water surrounds the small square base of his throne on all sides; a distant ship rides the waves. As ruler of the element Water, the King of Cups can naturally be associated with the mythological king of oceans, Poseidon (Neptune).

D ivinatory meaning: A perceptive, creative, generous person. A distinguished and accomplished character. One in peril at times of being thrown off balance by the power of their emotions. Someone given to tempestuous outbursts and stormy relationships, but also one capable of still depths and a fluid emotional authenticity.

ĄCE OF COINS

64-1, *Ship of Fools Tarot*

fool strains to pull two carts, the second of which holds an enormous coin (64-1). In the *Narrenschiff* original, for "Of the path of
righteousness" (*Von dem weg der selligkeit**), both carts are empty and
the second, representing the cart of heaven, rides in flames (64-2).
The *Tarot de Marseille* ace accentuates the flat and decorative aspect of

---

*   Of the Path of Righteousness: "Many insist on following the way of foolishness /
    And pull behind them a heavy cart, / And yet the righteous path would lead
    closer to heaven."

64-2, *Narrenschiff*

64-3, *Tarot de Marseille*

64-4, *Rider-Waite Tarot*

Minor Arcana 171

the single coin (64-3). Scrollwork and flowers frame it. The Ace of Pentacles of the *Waite-Smith* series shows a large, heavenly hand that holds a disk inscribed with a five-pointed star or pentagram (64-4). The hand and pentacle float above a lush garden in which a shrubbery arch opens on distant mountains.

Coins are the suit of the material and concrete, of the element Earth. Earth is the heaviest element, the most stable; also, the coldest and least flexible. The earthy element therefore fosters an admirable stability, philosophical clarity, and practicality, but also melancholy and materialism. Commerce, property, resources, and wealth are also the business of the suit of coins.

Divinatory meaning: Tangible success, prosperity, financial security, solid foundations. Physical health, philosophical precision, spiritual well-being. Real wealth, big money. If reversed or inauspiciously placed, the card can represent a mistaken emphasis on material wealth—or on materialism of any kind. Wealth can be a burden as well as a boon.

65 — Two of Coins

TWO OF COINS

65-1, *Ship of Fools Tarot*

A cheerful fool stands in a city street and holds two large coins in his outstretched arms (65-1). In the original image three crows perch on the fool's hands and head, each crying the word "*cras,*" Latin for "tomorrow" (65-2). Here Brant takes to task those fools who prolong their folly, who postpone abandoning their foolish ways. The *Narrenschiff* figure, for "Of seeking delay" (*Von vffschlag suchen**), has

---

*   Of Seeking Delay: "He who crows 'caw, caw' just like a raven / Remains a fool until the grave; / Tomorrow he will don an even larger dunce's cap."

been borrowed for his resemblance to the *Waite-Smith* card: a juggler in a high hat holding out two pentacles, which are bound together by a figure-eight ribbon (65-3). Two tiny ships ride high waves in the distance. The Two of Coins represents the dynamic balance of opposing or complementary forces. The juggler's game is an echo of the cosmic dance of all matter: rising and falling, becoming and ending.

Divinatory meaning: Dynamic equilibrium, balance in movement. Conflicting demands brought into a tenuous harmony. A difficult juggling act; a graceful performance. Danger of dropping the ball, of having too many plates in the air; the promise of equipoise.

65-2, *Narrenschiff*

65-3, *Rider-Waite Tarot*

66 — Three of Coins

THREE OF COINS

66-1, *Ship of Fools Tarot*

Three workmen stride away as a seated fool tears his hair in alarm on the Three of Coins card (66-1). The three coins are actually circular openings in a gothic window in the unfinished wall at the back of the scene. These three circles and the removal of a cup from the table in front of the fool are the only changes made from the *Narrenschiff* image, in which Brant mocks fools who build without plans, who spend without budgeting, who charge ahead without looking forward (*Von narrechtem anslag**) (66-2). In the *Waite-Smith* version a workman pauses at his stone carving to speak with a tonsured priest and a hooded boy. Above them gothic tracery describes three pentacles (66-3). The Three of Coins card manifests ideas of building, of skill, and of mastery.

Divinatory meaning: Great plans, big setback. Architects, builders, and workmen mean: anguish. Constructive ambitions, ambitious constructions. No monument is built without delays and obstacles: success requires risk.

---

* Of Foolish Designs: "He who would build without regard / Of what costs are required / Will find himself at the end before he begins."

66-2, *Narrenschiff*   66-3, *Rider-Waite Tarot*

67 — Four of Coins

FOUR OF COINS

67-1, *Ship of Fools Tarot*

greedy fool counts out on one hand the sum he is exacting from a poor fellow who reaches into his purse to pay (67-1). The image has been altered from the original, on usury and profiteering (*Wucher vnd furkouff* *), primarily in the substitution of four large coins for the innumerable small ones in his tall sacks (67-2). Two barrels crowd the village street behind them. On the *Waite-Smith* card, a solitary king

---

* Usury and Exploitation: "The usurers perpetrate a vile trade / And prey upon the poor / Without heed, that in so doing / They starve the world."

enfolds a pentacle in his arms while one more rides above his head and two more lie under each foot (67-3). In the distance rise the many towers of a medieval town, resembling the cityscape of San Gimignano in Italy's Province of Siena.

Divinatory meaning: Attachment to money, a love of material goods, avarice, greed. Difficulties in business, professional disagreements. Valuable lesson learned from a hard transaction. A fool and his money are soon parted.

67-2, Narrenschiff

67-3, Rider-Waite Tarot

68 — *Five of Coins*

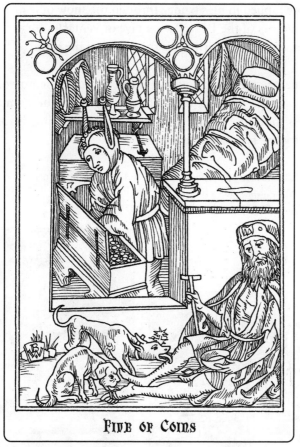

FIVE OF COINS

68-1, *Ship of Fools Tarot*

A wealthy fool, standing in a well-furnished bedchamber, paws through a chest full of treasure in the Five of Coins (68-1). Another chest stands closed, a shelf holds plate and ewers, in the corner stands a bed. In the street outside an old beggar sits with his crutch and begging bowl. Two dogs lick at his wounds, as the poor soul is too weak to resist them. Once again the only difference from the *Narrenschiff* original, for "Of Useless Riches" (*Von vnnutzem rich-tum**), is in the addition of the five suit signs, which have been inte-grated into the fool's arched windows (68-2). A crippled beggar and a woman wrapped in rags trudge through the snow outside the stained glass windows of the *Waite-Smith* Five of Pentacles (68-3). Impover-ishment, actual and spiritual, is the theme of the card.

Divinatory meaning: Poverty: either the actual penury of the beg-gar; or the spiritual destitution of the rich and complacent. If money is short, the card instructs patience; if plentiful, it admonishes to charity and sympathy for others.

---

* Of Useless Riches: "He who has riches, and delights in them, / Paying no heed to those in need, / Will be forsaken, so that he too shall beg."

68-2, *Narrenschiff*

68-3, *Rider-Waite Tarot*

69 — Six of Coins

69-1, *Ship of Fools Tarot*

SIX OF COINS

bearded fool stands in an open landscape, holding an enormous balance and scales in one hand and a large coin in the other (69-1). Five similar coins lie in the bowls of the scales. The image from which the card has been adapted, "Disdain of Eternal Joy" (*Verachtung ewiger freyt**), lacks the large coins, while contrasting small objects are

---

* Disdain of Eternal Joy: "Because I place such stock in the mundane, / And disregard that which is eternal, / I have made a monkey of myself."

weighed against each other (69-2). For Brant, this is an image of the fool who chooses temporal things over eternal ones. The corresponding *Waite-Smith* card shows an expensively dressed burgher who dispenses coins to a pair of kneeling mendicants with one hand and holds the balance and scales with the other (69-3). The scales of justice have, in this card, been tipped to beneficence and largesse.

Divinatory meaning: Charity and philanthropy; generosity and benevolence. Gifts and aid that are unstinting but also measured and considered. The scales of justice can also be those of charity. If ill favored, the card may signal charity parsimoniously doled out.

69-2, *Narrenschiff*

69-3, *Rider-Waite Tarot*

70 — Seven of Coins

70-1, *Ship of Fools Tarot*

Two energetic fools push and pull a plow on the card of the Seven of Coins (70-1). A falcon perches on the hand of one. Seven coins, like large round fruit, hang in the canopy of a stand of trees beyond the field being tilled by the two men. The seven hanging disks are the only important departure from the *Narrenschiff* illustration, used for both "Of ignoring good counsel" (*Nit volgen gutem ratt**) and

---

* Of Ignoring Good Counsel: "He who cannot say yes or no / And pays no heed to advice large and small, / He will pay for it alone."

"Of persisting in the good" (*Von beharren jn gutem***) (70-2). The corresponding *Waite-Smith* card shows a young man who pauses in his farming or gardening to rest on his hoe and gaze at the fruit of his labors: seven pentacles that tumble like gourds amidst a broad-leafed vine (70-3). Fruitfulness and worthy effort are the subject of this card.

Divinatory meaning: Productive labor, fruitful undertaking. The satisfactions of growing things, of farming and gardening. The pleasure of sowing and tending; the enjoyment of seeing the bud and then the bloom; the reward and repose of harvest. Also, the suspense and uncertainty of the harvest, when one week's weather may determine an entire season's success. Thus, the patience and hopefulness of the true farmer. Reaping what you sow: plant corn, get corn.

** Of Persisting in the Good: "Many men grip the plow tightly / And yet end in woe nonetheless, / For the cuckoo stays in his nest."

70-2, *Narrenschiff*

70-3, *Rider-Waite Tarot*

71 — Eight of Coins

71-1, *Ship of Fools Tarot*

On one knee and wielding a mallet, a fool works on one of eight large coins in his open-air workshop (71-1). Two coins lie on the ground, five more hang at the edge of a wall. Our image is, of course, based on the *Waite-Smith* model, in which a craftsman seated on a workbench hammers the pentagram pattern into one of eight disks (71-2). Honest labor and craftsmanship are the motif of the Eight of Coins.

Divinatory meaning: The satisfaction of working with one's own hands. Old arts, new hobbies. The work of the artist, artisan, craftsman. Creativity, productivity, proficiency, virtuosity. Dignified work, not always dignified with commensurate remuneration.

71-2, *Rider-Waite Tarot*

72 — Nine of Coins

NINE OF COINS

72-1, *Ship of Fools Tarot*

𝕬 company of four fools, two female and two male, play a hand of cards on the Nine of Coins (72-1). Their game takes place in a room or alcove that opens on one side to a city street. A fool's cap hangs on the far wall. One male fool has his hand at the waist of his neighbor; the image mocks the dalliance of lovers as well as the folly of gamblers (*Von spylern**). Only the addition of nine coins to the

---

* Of Gamblers: "Many so dearly love to gamble / That they seek no other entertainment / And pay no heed to their future losses."

round table top sets the image apart from the *Narrenschiff* original (72-2). In contrast the *Waite-Smith* card portrays a single graceful female figure strolling in a garden (72-3). She rests one hand on a flower-bound pentacle, one among nine. A hooded hunting bird perches on her other, gloved, hand. Her robes are long and flowing, a bonnet of Tudor style frames her face. As different as are the two versions of the card, they both announce pleasure and ease.

Divinatory meaning: Conviviality and festivity. Pleasure, enjoyment, ease. Dinner parties, party games. Courtship and flirtation. Games and gambling. Carousing, excess, and risk taking.

72-2, *Narrenschiff*

72-3, *Rider-Waite Tarot*

TEN OF COINS

73-1, *Ship of Fools Tarot*

ale and female fools dance and parade around a column surmounted by a statue of the biblical golden calf (73-1). The
image comes directly from Brant's book, from an illustration that criticizes mindless cavorting and lascivious dancing (*Von dantzen**) (73-
2). As usual, the main difference is the interpolation of coins into the

---

* Of Dancing: "Of dancing this at least may be said / That one does not always
  plow ahead / But may also turn and wheel back."

scene: in the hands of the fools, in the capital of the column, in the upper corners of the frame. The *Waite-Smith* Ten of Pentacles shows an old man seated in profile, a graceful dancing couple, a small child, and two dogs (73-3). A dark arch frames a distant tower, battlements, and treetops. The ten pentacles themselves float in a symmetrical foreground pattern. The Ten of Coins is a card that promises pleasure and celebration.

Divinatory meaning: Dancing and dallying, courting and coupling. Parties, celebration, revelry, jubilation. Neglecting serious matters for immediate pleasures.

73-2, *Narrenschiff*

73-3, *Rider-Waite Tarot*

74 — Page of Coins

PAGE OF COINS

74-1, *Ship of Fools Tarot*

Geese surround a cheerful fool on the Page of Coins card (74-1). Only the coin itself differs from the original *Narrenschiff* woodcut, for "Fools now as before" (*Narr hur als vern**) (74-2). The *Marseille* page is a standing young man with a coin in his right hand (74-3). Another coin stands at his feet. Pamela Colman Smith's Page

---

* Fools Now as Before: "Many fancy themselves great wits / And yet are geese to a man, / All refinement and reason they disdain."

74-2, *Narrenschiff*

74-3, *Tarot de Marseille*

74-4, *Rider Waite Tarot*

of Pentacles lightly balances his disk on his fingertips (74-4). He is elegantly dressed and wears a large hat with a trailing drape.

Divinatory meaning: A smart, even intellectual person; pragmatic and responsible, but also with a mystical, mysterious side. A student of the earth, delighted with nature's abundance—as the birds surrounding him fascinate the page.

75 — Knight of Coins

KNIGHT OF COINS

75-1, *Ship of Fools Tarot*

The Knight of Coins rides a crowned pig (75-1). He smiles, holds his emblematic coin, and holds the reins of the animal. There is no single source in the *Narrenschiff* for the *Ship of Fools* image, but the sow comes from an illustration that accompanies the chapter that condemns crude language (*Von groben narren**) (75-2). The *Tarot de*

---

* Of Vulgar Fools: "Vile and scandalous words irritate / And are sure to destroy our good manners / If we always let the sow's bell ring."

75-2, *Narrenschiff*

75-3, *Tarot de Marseille*

75-4, *Rider-Waite Tarot*

Marseille offers us a Knight of Coins who rides a horse and holds a staff, while his coin is suspended in the air above him (75-3). The *Waite-Smith* knight sits very still on his dark horse (75-4). He wears full Renaissance armor, including a plumed helmet, and holds the expected suit sign.

Divinatory meaning: A dedicated, diligent, industrious person. A researcher or scholar, an explorer or trailblazer. A determined traveler, with a sense of humor, more concerned with the journey than with the elegance of his conveyance.

76 — *Queen of Coins*

QUEEN OF COINS

76-1, Ship of Fools Tarot

The Queen of Coins, an attractive woman in a tight bodice and a high hat, sits on a curious perch: a long paddle held by a wild-eyed demon (76-1). This bird-clawed monster is about to move the unconcerned beauty onto the flaming grill in the foreground. The original *Narrenschiff* image shows the woman holding up a mirror;

76-2, *Narrenschiff*

76-3, *Tarot de Marseille*

76-4, *Rider-Waite Tarot*

she is an emblem of human vanity and pride (*Vberhebung der hoch-fart**) (76-2). The seated *Tarot de Marseille* queen holds high her coin and leans a scepter on her shoulder (76-3). She wears the expected crown and has sweeping sleeves. Similarly seated and regally dressed is the Queen of Pentacles designed by Pamela Colman Smith (76-4). Her richly carved stone throne is embellished on the arms with small ram's heads. She cradles her pentacle in her lap and leans down pensively toward it. Her crown, with its long sheer veil, is almost Russian in taste. All around her are flowers and trailing leaves. At one side a distant landscape can be seen, at the other a rabbit hops into the scene. Demeter (Ceres) is a goddess who can cast light on the Queen of Coins, for she too is a figure of generosity, fertility, and industry. An even better fit, though, may be her daughter Persephone (Proserpina), the maiden who becomes, after her abduction by the king of Tartarus, queen of the Underworld.

Divinatory meaning: An individual grounded, practical, sensible, but also generous, dignified, creative, and courtly. One who runs the risk of being attached to the physical or material, to beauty or luxury. But the queen is an earth mother; a well-rooted, fruitful, blooming personage.

---

* Overestimation of Pride: "She who is arrogant, and praises herself / And wishes to sit alone on high / She the devil sets upon his claws."

77 — King of Coins

King of Coins

77-1, Ship of Fools Tarot

The King of Coins is a kneeling man who shows himself, with his prominent asses' ears, to be Midas (77-1). The original *Narrenschiff* image shows him praying, without coin and crown, that his golden touch be revoked (*Von vnutzem wunschen**) (77-2). The *Tarot de Marseille* king sits cross-legged and holds his coin at his knee (77-3).

---

* Of Idle Wishes: "He who wishes for that after which he has not striven / And puts not his stock in God, / He will come to great grief and scorn."

77-2, *Narrenschiff*

77-3, *Tarot de Marseille*

77-4 *Rider-Waite Tarot*

He wears the large crowned hat so typical of the *Marseille* images. The *Waite-Smith* King of Pentacles shows another type (77-4). He too is seated, but he wears heavy flowing robes decorated with grape clusters. He rests his large disk on his left knee and holds a short scepter in his right hand. Carved bull's heads and floral garlands adorn his dark throne. Vines and flowers surround him; even his crown is trimmed with bloom.

Midas was a wise man who became a fool in his impetuous love of gold; but prayers and knowledge redeemed him. The King of Coins recalls other mythological personages tied to the element Earth and to earthiness: Pluto, especially as god of hidden riches; and even Dionysus (Bacchus), god of the vine and thus of Earth's richness and fertility.

Divinatory meaning: A successful person, with the problems as well as pleasures that this affords. An earthy, solid, grounded person. A businesslike, systematic, efficient person; an effective manager and leader. A person susceptible, at times, to depend too much on ideas of pragmatism and material success.

Reading the Cards

Many customs and traditions have grown up around the use of tarot cards for divination or meditation. This writer encourages the reader to feel free to embrace or reject, to pick and choose one's rites and rituals. You may opt to keep your cards wrapped in a special cloth, or in a small decorated case. In preparation for a reading, some prefer to put the cards in order before shuffling them thoroughly.

In keeping with the spirit of a tarot composed of fools, some lighthearted approaches can be taken. In addition to shuffling the cards in the usual way, they might be tucked into a hat and then carefully tossed before being drawn, one by one, as a sleight-of-hand magician draws a rabbit from a top hat.

Another way to begin would entail first marking out an area on a floor or a table, perhaps by laying down a favorite scarf, and then throwing the cards high in the air. Read those that land faceup in your designated circle or square—a reminder of the first card game learned by children, "fifty-two-card pick-up."

Pulling cards from a hat recalls the techniques of such Dadaist poets as Tristan Tzara, who composed his works by depending on such chance juxtapositions. Another technique inspired by Dadaism and surrealism would be a card spread based loosely on the idea of the game called the "Exquisite Corpse," in which passages of a story are written separately and then united, or body parts of a figure drawing are sketched independently and then joined. This spread works best with as many readers as there are individual cards chosen, but it can also be adapted for a single reader. With as many as six readers, a reading would be structured thus: a first reader chooses a card for the feet, which represents the foundation of the current situation. It tells what kind of ground the querent stands upon. A second reader then chooses a card for the thighs, a card that can tell what forces are helping to propel the querent forward, or which ones may be holding her back. A third reader chooses a card for the groin, which tells of libido, desire, and pleasure. A fourth reader takes a card for the belly, which speaks to issues of health, stability, and practicality. Finances and work are also lodged here, for without a full stomach all other considerations can seem secondary. A fifth reader then chooses a card for the heart, where the deepest emotional considerations, especially those that touch on love, are weighed. Finally a sixth reader selects a last card, for the head. In addition to pointing toward a final answer for the reading, the card also touches on topics of the mind and the soul. The Exquisite Corpse works most Dadaistically when several different readers determine independently what each card means, and then bring their interpretations together to enjoy the undoubtedly odd ensemble, but the spread also adapts easily to use by a single reader.

The best-known card spread is called the Celtic Cross. There are several published variations in the arrangement of the cards in the Celtic Cross. Herewith is the sequence that I have followed.

Card 1: *Today,* placed at the center, upright, tells of the current situation of the querent.

Card 2: *Tomorrow,* placed above and crossing the first, is the immediate situation or atmosphere into which the querent moves.

Card 3: *Above You,* placed above the previous two, shows the desires, goals, or perhaps fears of the querent.

Card 4: *Behind You,* placed to one side of the central cards, is a distant past foundation that contributes to the present situation.

Card 5: Below You, placed below the central cards, shows recent past influences and incidents.

Card 6: Before You, placed to the opposite side of card 4, shows forces or influences to come.

Card 7: You, placed to the right of the cross, at the bottom, represents the querent.

Card 8: House, placed above card 7, reveals the environment, work and home, of the querent.

Card 9: Heart, placed above the former two cards, tells something of the inner state of the questioner.

Card 10: Harvest, placed atop the others, suggests an answer or final result.

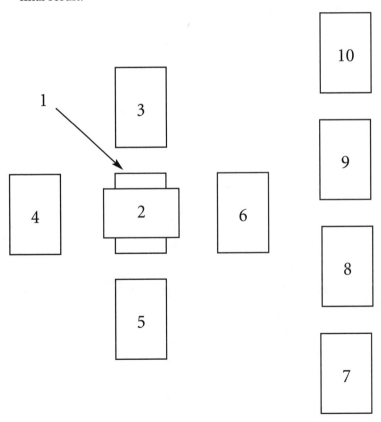

Bibliography

Brant, Sebastian, *The Ship of Fools,* translated by
Alexander Barclay, edited by T. H. Jamieson
(Edinburgh and London, 1874). Barclay's 1509
adaptation of Brant (not a proper translation, as it
was dependent on Latin and French intermediaries)
influenced the course of English letters.

Williams, Brian. *A Renaissance Tarot.* U.S. Games
Systems, Inc. (Stamford, Conn., 1994). Discusses tarot
symbolism in detail, especially in the context of
European medieval and Renaissance art.

Schultz, Franz. *Sebastian Brant, Das Narrenschiff*
(Strassburg, 1913). Excellent facsimile edition of
the first Basel edition of 1494.

Zarncke, Friedrich, (editor). *Sebastian Brant, Das
Narrenschiff* (Leipzig, 1854). A definitive classic
critical edition of the *Narrenschiff.*

Zeydel, Edwin H. *The Ship of Fools by Sebastian Brants,*
translation with commentary (Columbia University
Press, 1944). Reprinted by Dover Publications (New
York, 1962); the essential modern popular source in
English for images and text.

☽ REACH FOR THE MOON

Llewellyn publishes hundreds of books on your favorite subjects! To get these exciting books, including the ones on the following pages, check your local bookstore or order them directly from Llewellyn.

Order by Phone
- Call toll-free within the U.S. and Canada, 1-877-NEW WRLD
- In Minnesota, call (651) 291-1970
- We accept VISA, MasterCard, and American Express

Order by Mail
- Send the full price of your order (MN residents add 7% sales tax) in U.S. funds, plus postage & handling to:

  Llewellyn Worldwide
  P.O. Box 64383, Dept. 0-7387-0161-0
  St. Paul, MN 55164-0383, U.S.A.

Postage & Handling
- **Standard** (U.S., Mexico, & Canada)

If your order is:
   $20.00 or under, add $5.00
   $20.01–$100.00, add $6.00
   Over $100, shipping is free

(Continental U.S. orders ship UPS. AK, HI, PR, & P.O. Boxes ship USPS 1st class. Mex. & Can. ship PMB.)

- **Second Day Air** (Continental U.S. only): $10.00 for one book + $1.00 per each additional book

- Express (AK, HI, & PR only) [Not available for P.O. Box delivery. For street address delivery only.]: $15.00 for one book + $1.00 per each additional book

- **International Surface Mail:** Add $1.00 per item

- **International Airmail:** Books—Add the retail price of each item; Non-book items—Add $5.00 per item

Please allow 4–6 weeks for delivery on all orders.
Postage and handling rates subject to change.

Discounts
We offer a 20% discount to group leaders or agents. You must order a minimum of 5 copies of the same book to get our special quantity price.

Free Catalog
Get a free copy of our color catalog, *New Worlds of Mind and Spirit.* Subscribe for just $10.00 in the United States and Canada ($30.00 overseas, airmail). Call 1-877-NEW WRLD today!

Visit our website at www.llewellyn.com for more information.

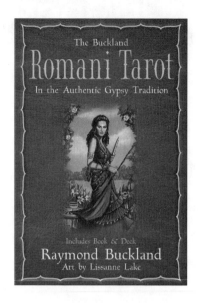

The Buckland Romani Tarot Kit

In the Authentic Gypsy Tradition

**Raymond Buckland
art by Lissanne Lake**

*The first Tarot to bring the ways
of the Gypsies to life.*

This tarot is based on Gypsies (Romanies) as the author knew them, growing up in England before and after World War II. They were colorful nomads, with their bright clothes and brilliantly painted wagons, or vardos. Following the traditional form of the Tarot—which was originally introduced into Europe by the Gypsies—this deck is unique in its use of Romani scenes to portray the ancient symbolism. Anyone who is familiar with the Tarot will enjoy the refreshing new approach, and anyone new to the cards will equally enjoy this rendition.

- Captures the Gypsy flavor in a deck of traditional Tarot cards
- Discover Raymond Buckland's own method of interpreting the cards
- Learn about the history of the Gypsies, their entry into Europe and Asia, and their introduction of the Tarot cards to the Western world

1-56718-099-X
Boxed Kit: 78-card deck and 6 x 9, 264-pp. illus. book   **$34.95**

Tarot: Your Everyday Guide

Practical Problem Solving and Everyday Advice

Janina Renée

Whenever people begin to read the tarot, they inevitably find themselves asking the cards, "What should I do about such-and-such situation?" Yet there is little information available on how to get those answers from the cards.

Reading the tarot for advice requires a different approach than reading for prediction, so the card descriptions in *Tarot: Your Everyday Guide* are adapted accordingly. You interpret a card in terms of things that you can do, and the central figure in the card, which usually represents the querent, models what ought to be done.

This book is especially concerned with practical matters, applying the tarot's advice to common problems and situations that many people are concerned about, such as whether to say "yes" or "no" to an offer, whether or not to become involved in some cause or conflict, choosing between job and educational options, starting or ending relationships, and dealing with difficult people.

1-56718-565-7, 7½ x 9⅛, 312 pp.   **$12.95**

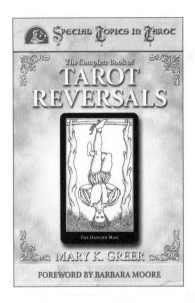

The Complete Book of Tarot Reversals

Mary K. Greer

*The topsy-turvy world of
upside-down cards*

What do you do with the "other half" of a Tarot reading: the reversed cards? Just ignore them as many people do? *Tarot Reversals* reveals everything you need to know for reading the most maligned and misunderstood part of a spread. These interpretations offer inner support, positive advice, and descriptions of the learning opportunities available, yet with a twist that is uniquely their own.

Enhance and deepen the quality of your consultations as you experiment with the eleven different methods of reading reversed cards. Use the author's interpretations to stimulate your own intuitive ideas. Struggle in the dark no longer.

- The author has a strong reputation with Tarot enthusiasts
- The first book to fully and exclusively address the interpretation of cards that appear upside-down in a Tarot spread
- Features eleven different methods of determining reversed card meanings
- For readers at all levels of expertise

1-56718-285-2, 6 x 9, 312 pp.   **$14.95**

The Nigel Jackson Tarot

Nigel Jackson

This breathtaking new tarot deck by world-renowned artist Nigel Jackson is a return to authentic medieval-renaissance symbolism and an amazing breakthrough in our knowledge of the authentic nature and meaning of the Tarot images.

For three centuries, scholars have speculated on the origins of the Tarot. Now Nigel Jackson presents his original theory concerning the medievalized Orphic-Pythagorean numerology underpinning of the cards, which could revolutionize our understanding of the Tarot and the secret tradition on which it lies.

The Neo-Pythagorean magical origin advanced by *The Nigel Jackson Tarot* is perhaps the first serious attempt in this century to reassess the Tarot tradition in a fresh and insightful way. It places this enigmatic oracle in its true context, that of late Graeco-Roman mystery-wisdom.

1-56718-365-4, Boxed Mini-Kit: 78-card deck and 160-pp. mini-book in slip case   **$24.95**

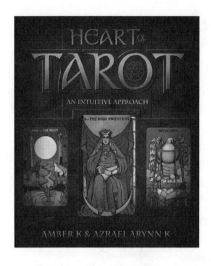

Heart of Tarot:
An Intuitive Approach
Amber K and Azrael K

An amazingly accurate technique for uncovering the Tarot's hidden messages

Heart of Tarot presents an entirely new way to read the Tarot that doesn't involve memorizing card meanings, using psychic skills, or learning obscure occult lore. Rather, it offers an amazingly accurate technique called "Gestalt Tarot," which is based on the principles of psychology. It is easy to learn and master.

A Gestalt Tarot reading does not provide vague, general information that's applicable to everyone. It gives you unique, personalized interpretations that apply only to you, or to the person who is receiving the reading. It is for those who truly want to know themselves better and take charge of their lives.

- Gestalt Tarot, based on sound psychological principles, helps bring pertinent information from the subconscious to the conscious mind

- The Gestalt Tarot technique enables you to uncover personalized information that applies to you and you alone

- It is a universal system that can be used with any Tarot deck

- This is a complete Tarot resource, with chapters on Tarot magick, teaching Tarot, and reading the cards professionally

1-56718-008-6, 7½ x 9⅛, 288 pp., 49 illus.   **$14.95**

Robin Wood Tarot Deck

created and illustrated by Robin Wood

instructions by Robin Wood & Michael Short

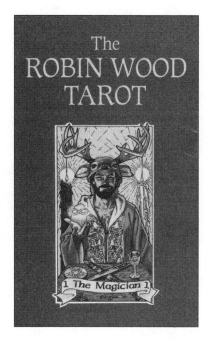

Tap into the wisdom of your sub-conscious with one of the most beautiful Tarot decks on the market today! Reminiscent of the Rider-Waite deck, the *Robin Wood Tarot* is flavored with nature imagery and luminous energies that will enchant you and the querant. Even the novice reader will find these cards easy and enjoyable to interpret.

Radiant and rich, these cards were illustrated with a unique technique that brings out the resplendent color of the prismacolor pencils. The shining strength of this Tarot deck lies in its depiction of the Minor Arcana. Unlike other Minor Arcana decks, this one springs to pulsating life. The cards are printed in quality card stock and boxed complete with instruction booklet, which provides the upright and reversed meanings of each card, as well as three basic card layouts. Beautiful and brilliant, the Robin Wood Tarot is a must-have deck!

0-87542-894-0, Boxed Kit: 78 cards with booklet $19.95

The Sacred Circle Tarot: A Celtic Pagan Journey

Anna Franklin
illustrated by Paul Mason

The Sacred Circle Tarot is a new concept in tarot design, combining photographs, computer imaging, and traditional drawing techniques to create stunning images. It draws on the Pagan heritage of Britain and Ireland, its sacred sites and landscapes. Key symbols unlock the deepest levels of Pagan teaching.

The imagery of the cards is designed to work on a number of levels, serving as a tool not only for divination but to facilitate meditation, personal growth, and spiritual development. The "sacred circle" refers to the progress of the initiate from undirected energy, through dawning consciousness, to the death of the old self and the emergence of the new.

The major arcana is modified somewhat to fit the pagan theme of the deck. For example, "The Fool" becomes "The Green Man," "The Heirophant" becomes "The Druid," and "The World" becomes "The World Tree." The accompanying book gives a full explanation of the symbolism in the cards and their divinatory meanings.

1-56718-457-X, Boxed Kit: 78 full-color cards;
6 x 9, 288-pp. book   **$29.95**

Victoria Regina Tarot

Sarah Ovenall & Georg Patterson

*A tarot of haunting beauty
and hidden surprises*

"To experience these images is to enter into a spellbinding parallel universe, an encompassing dream world."
    —Brian Williams, creator of the
Renaissance Tarot

With the poignancy of visions com-bined with an element of nostalgic humor, the Victoria Regina Tarot brings to life the fascinating art of engravings used in late nineteenth-century commercial illustration.

    Victoria Regina Tarot is the work of collage done in black and white, providing a sepia-tinted glimpse into another time, yet containing messages for our time. See the Devil depicted as an evil clown and the Chariot as a woman on a bicycle. Justice holds a handgun and a postage scale. Cups have become Mason jars, Rods are fountain pens, Discs are pocket watches, and Swords are handguns. Historical figures (mostly members of the Royal Family) grace the court cards.

- The only Victorian tarot currently available
- Connects the meanings of the cards with moments or figures from nineteenth-century British history
- The accompanying guidebook includes a description of each card, its interpretation, and notes on the sources
- For tarot enthusiasts and collectors of all things Victorian

**1-56718-531-2, Boxed Kit: 78-card deck, velvet bag,
6 x 9, 264-pp. illustrated guidebook**   **$34.95**

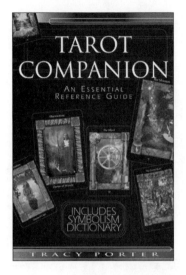

The Tarot Companion: An Essential Reference Guide

Tracy Porter

While some people are so psychically gifted they can give an accurate tarot reading without any formal training, most of us need to develop our inherent intuition. The first step in doing that is to study the symbolism imbedded in the cards. This book is a complete reference to those symbols for all readers, beginning through advanced.

The different symbol systems covered in this book include the following: (1) astrology, which was central to the development of the Major Arcana; (2) numerology which is fundamental to understanding the tarot as each card was placed in its sequence for a particular reason; (3) cabala, which is essential if you want to progress from novice to the more advanced stages; (4) the I-Ching and runes, which evolved separately from the tarot, but which can help you align harmoniously with world-wide philosophies; (5) colors and chakras, which will help you understand the nuances in the scenes and the backgrounds.

1-56718-574-6, 5³⁄₁₆ x 8, 264 pp. $12.95

Tarot for a
New Generation

Janina Renée

The only tarot manual targeted
to-ward young adults and their
concerns. Studies, career plan-
ning, driver's licenses, friends,
acceptance and popularity, romance, family relationships—
these are just some of the issues
that occupy the minds of today's
young people.

Tarot for a New Generation is the first instructional guide to tarot
reading that speaks to the concerns of the sixteen- to twenty-five-
year-old age group. While fun to read and use, it is for young adults
and beginners who are serious about training their intuition and lead-
ing more examined lives. It presents a symbol system that they can
work with to help plan their life paths and make a place for themselves in the world.

- The only book to explore how the Tarot responds to issues
  important to young people ages sixteen to twenty-five

- Includes a section on Tarot visualizations for help with
  studies, building self-confidence, dealing with parents,
  healing, and more

- Promotes ethical standards and a positive approach to
  interpretation without being preachy

0-7387-0160-2, 7½ x 9⅛, 416 pp., illus.   **$14.95**

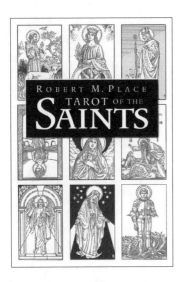

Tarot of the Saints
Robert M. Place

*A beautiful blending
of two traditions*

Saints lend themselves remarkably well to correspondences with the archetypal images of the Tarot—St. Francis: a Fool for Christ; St. Nicholas: the Miracle Worker (Magician); St. Mary Magdalen: The First Papesse (High Priestess). Saints serve as examples of ideal behavior, values, and outlook. By nature they are well-suited to dispense insight and wisdom through the cards. Whether historical or mythical, their personalities bring life to the abstract images of the Tarot.

The accompanying guidebook provides the history and legend of each saint, insights into the Tarot, and explanations of the cards and how to use them. This is the only Tarot deck of saints ever produced, by an award-winning artist and recognized expert on the history and philosophy of the Tarot.

**ISBN 1-56718-527-4, Boxed kit: 78 full-color cards
and 6 x 9, 264-pp. book**   **$34.95**

To Order, Call 1-877-NEW WRLD
Prices subject to change without notice